Oliver Cromwell

David Sharp

ANTHAM COL' EGE LIBRARY

D0190861

Heinemann

Heinemann Educational Publishers
Halley Court, Jordan Hill, Oxford OX2 8EJ
Part of Harcourt Education Limited

Heinemann is the registered trademark of Harcourt Education Limited

First published 2003

07 06 05 04 03
10 9 8 7 6 5 4 3 2 1

British Library Cataloguing in Publication Data is available from the British
Library on request.

ISBN 0 435 32756 9

Designed and typeset by Wyvern 21 Ltd

Printed and bound in the UK by The Bath Press Ltd

Index compiled by Ian D. Crane

Photographic acknowledgements
The author and publisher would like to thank the following for permission to
reproduce photographs: Bridgeman/Houses of Parliament, Westminster: p. 16;
Bridgeman/Leeds Museums & Galleries: p. 3; Bridgeman/Private Collection: p. 5,
35; Collections Picture Library: p. 10; Fotomas Index: p. 59; Hulton: p. 41; Mary
Evans: p. 9, 25; National Portrait Gallery: p. 15, 57.

Cover photograph: © AKG

Picture research by Bea Thomas

Written acknowledgements
The author and publisher gratefully acknowledge the following publications from
which written sources in the book are drawn.
W.C. Abbott, *Writings and Speeches of Cromwell* (Cambridge, 1937): p.95-6;
G.E. Alymer, *Rebellion or Revolution?* (OUP, 1986): p.84; T. Barnard, *The English
Republic* (Longman, 1982): p.85; R. Baxter, *The Autobiography of Richard Baxter*,
ed. N.H. Keeble (Dent, 1974): p.77; S. Bethel, *The World's Mistake in Oliver
Cromwell* (Northcote House, 1972); p.78; G. Burnet, *History of His Own Time*
(London, 1724): p.79; E.H. Clarendon, *History of the Great Rebellion*, ed. W.D.
Macray (Clarenden Press, 1992): p.76, 99; B. Coward, *Oliver Cromwell*
(Longman, 1991): p. 84, 100, 104; C. Hill, *God's Englishman* (Penguin, 1972):
p.83; C. Hill, *Oliver Cromwell* (London, 1958): p.101,104; D. Hirst, *Authority
and Conflict* (Arnold, 1986): p.99; L. Hutchinson, *Memoirs of the Life of Colonel
Hutchinson*, ed. N.H. Keeble (Phoenix, 2000): p.78; R. Hutton, *The British
Republic* (Macmillan, 2000): p.83; J.P. Kenyon (ed), *The Stuart Constitution*
(CUP, 1986): pp.86-9, 89-91; I. Roots (ed), *Speeches of Oliver Cromwell* (Dent,
1989): p.91-4; D.L. Smith, *Oliver Cromwell a great Parliamentarian?* In
Cromwelliana (Journal of the Cromwell Association, 1995): p.82; C.V.
Wedgwood, *Oliver Cromwell* (Duckworth, 1973): p.104; A. Woolrych, *England
without a king* (Methuen, 1983): p.99; A. Woolrych, *The Cromwellian
Protectorate: A Military Dictatorship?* in History, 244 (Macmillan, 1990): p.86,
102.

CONTENTS

HOW TO USE THIS BOOK

This book has been written for students studying Oliver Cromwell at A level. It is specifically designed to cater for those students who are studying Cromwell and his impact as part of their A2 course. The sections have been written in such a way as to meet the demands of A level specifications and address some of the problems faced by students studying the seventeenth century.

The first section is a descriptive analysis. It outlines the background to Cromwell's life and explains the main events of his lifetime. The aim of this part of the book is to give students information that they can use to inform their interpretations about the main features of Cromwellian rule.

Sections 2 to 8 analyse some of the main questions about Cromwell. Certain key themes have been identified to lead students into debate. It is important to read Section 1 of the book before these sections because a certain understanding of events is necessary. These sections are not solely for students studying the topic at A2. AS students may read them to extend their knowledge and deepen their understanding of the topic.

Section 9 deals with the evidence of the period. Historians can have problems in deciphering the language of the seventeenth century, so these chapters provide students with help in dealing with primary evidence. To this end there are a number of examples of sources taken from the seventeenth century; these are accompanied by a commentary.

After Section 9 there is an assessment section that gives advice for students taking examinations for any of the three English examination boards.

The book assumes that students already have some background knowledge of this period although, of course, information is provided about Cromwell and his times in Section 1. Students should also read *England in Crisis, 1640–1660* by David Sharp (Heinemann 2000).

PART 1: CONTEXT AND KEY THEMES

SECTION 1

The 1620s and 1630s, and the early life of Oliver Cromwell

KEY THEMES

- Oliver Cromwell cannot be assessed without understanding that his attitudes, opinions and character were shaped by the political and religious crises in which he lived.
- Cromwell was over 40 before he became a national figure. His life as an average minor country gentleman and his deep permanent religious conversion are keys to understanding his contradictory and complex character.

INTRODUCTION

Oliver Cromwell is one of the central figures of English (and indeed British) history. His contribution to the unique events of the period 1640–58 – when England experienced three civil wars, an attempt to create a form of parliamentary democracy by a minority of radicals, the execution of King Charles I in 1649, and various republican regimes – was pivotal. By the end of 1653 he was Lord Protector – the only non-royal head of state in English history. It is not surprising that Cromwell has been the subject of more biographies than any other English soldier and politician. Nor is it surprising that there are many different views about him.

Put simply, here was an obscure country gentleman who became the first soldier of his age, defeating all he encountered – Royalists, Scots, Irish. He helped to prevent a radical group in his own army seizing power and creating a political revolution. He was a driving force behind the trial and execution of the anointed King of England as an 'enemy of the people'. He eventually ruled England for five years, holding a divided country together.

For some contemporaries and historians, his career is one of devious manoeuvres and self-seeking, a man responsible for destroying the legal monarchy in his quest for power, and a man prepared to change his principles. For others, he is the hero of the 'English Revolution', who destroyed dictatorial divine right monarchy and established 'English liberties'. Some have seen him as a religious bigot intent on creating a 'new Jerusalem' in England, peopled with Puritan killjoys; others, as a conservative dictator whose principal motivation was fear of anarchy.

Although foreign affairs are not dealt with in this volume, it could be said that Cromwell's army and navy were the most formidable in Europe. Blake and Monck, the greatest fighting seamen of their age, led the navy to a remarkable string of victories and helped to make England a 'great power' for the first time. The contemporary Royalist historian Lord Clarendon remarked that Cromwell's 'greatness at home was but a shadow of his greatness abroad'. After the Restoration, contemporaries remarking on Charles II's naval and military failures compared them with Cromwell's successes. When George Downing complained of being treated with less respect as Charles II's ambassador to France than as Cromwell's ambassador, he was told by the French 'but you were a great power then'.

What is certain is that his personality and achievements have cast a spell over English history, and that as a soldier he is seen as one of the great commanders, as well as a thoroughgoing English patriot. During 1940, when invasion seemed imminent, one of his admirers, Winston Churchill, chose 'Cromwell' as the codeword for all British forces, regular and Home Guard, to go to full alert.

Cromwell remains an enigma – his career, his own statements and actions open to differing interpretations – and any biography of him must leave questions unanswered. Two contemporary assessments of him illustrate the difficulty. The Royalist historian Lord Clarendon, in his monumental work *A History of the Great Rebellion* described him as a 'brave bad man'. His servant John Maidston, who perhaps saw more of Cromwell than any other and from a perspective that does not encourage hero-worship, said 'a larger soul hath seldom dwelt in a house of clay'.

Another problem associated with an assessment of Cromwell's life and achievements is that historians tend to interpret the past through the eyes of the present. Thus, after the 'republican experiment' had collapsed into anarchy in 1660, the restoration of Charles II was seen by many as deliverance. Cromwell was generally vilified and denigrated in histories written in the period 1660–1800. In the nineteenth century his part in destroying divine right monarchy and his belief in religious toleration made him a hero to nonconformist liberals who saw him as a force for 'progress', progress that was defined for them in terms of a gradual extension of parliamentary democracy and religious freedom.

In the twentieth century, Marxist historians such as Christopher Hill attacked him for missing or blocking the opportunity to create a democratic state. At the opposite end of the political spectrum, some right-wing historians praised him as a conservative dictator who saved England from anarchy. All these assessments suffer from the error of putting contemporary concepts into the minds and conditions of the seventeenth century. Whatever Cromwell was, he was a product of his times, shaped by the religious and political strife of the seventeenth century.

CROMWELL'S PERSONALITY AND CHARACTER

The key to assessing Cromwell's motives and actions lies in his background, beliefs and personality. He was a complex, contradictory character whose actions often seemed to go against his previous conduct and statements.

Oliver Cromwell.

The 1620s and 1630s, and the early life of Oliver Cromwell 3

A country gentleman

In some ways Cromwell was a conservative minor country gentleman, typical of his class and age. He looked back to a 'golden age' of order and stability with a balance between Crown and Parliament and a Church of England unsullied by Laudian high-church ideas. This period was the reign of Elizabeth I for whom he expressed admiration. Of course, his view of Elizabeth's reign was, to say the least, rose-tinted. As a country gentleman, he saw himself as part of a class that made up the natural rulers of the countryside: men of substance, but unsullied by court politics and the high living of some of the aristocracy. 'I was by birth a gentleman living in no great height, nor yet in obscurity' was how he put it. In other words, Cromwell saw the gentry as the backbone of the country. However, he seems to have taken his social responsibilities seriously, having a genuine concern for the poor, an interest in law reform to prevent the rich oppressing the poor, and a belief in charity.

Fear of anarchy

This does not mean that he was in any sense of the word a social revolutionary. He did believe in promotion by merit in the army he created, which to many contemporaries was shocking. A Parliamentarian Denzil Holles said 'most of the colonels and officers [are] mear tradesmen ... a notable dunghill if one would rake into it.' However, promotion by merit for Cromwell was merely common sense, showing a lack of prejudice rather than a desire to create a revolutionary 'army of the people'. When the radical group, the Levellers, whose programme included the vote for all men over 21, confronted Cromwell in the Putney Debates in 1647, he had no intention of implementing their revolutionary ideas. One of the mainsprings of his political thought was a fear of anarchy and the Leveller proposals would lead to anarchy in his eyes. Property would be under threat and the rule of the mob would follow.

Opponent of royal authority

At the other end of the spectrum, Cromwell found himself opposing royal authority on several grounds. First, in his view, King Charles I was trying to set up royal absolutism and destroy the fundamental freedoms of the subject in English common law. Second, he was destroying the balance between Parliament, which represented the men of property in the nation, and the power of the Crown. Third, as a Puritan, Cromwell saw Charles' support for the high-church Laudian changes to the Church of England as not only destroying the tolerant broad church of the Elizabethan church settlement, but a 'design to bring in popery'.

Believer in religious toleration

In religious terms, Cromwell can be seen as quite radical. He genuinely believed in religious toleration in an age that took the view that society could not be held together without a state church that enforced conformity. Thus, he opposed the narrow conformity that Laud tried to force on the Church of England. In the same way he opposed the majority in Parliament when they wished to replace the Church of England with a narrow Presbyterian church that all must attend. What was behind this quite remarkable adherence to religious toleration?

Cromwell believed that God would work through different people and that no one person could have a monopoly on the truth of God. To persecute Christians who did not agree with every point of doctrine might mean persecuting someone who, like Cromwell himself, had undergone a profound religious conversion.

BACKGROUND TO THE BREAKDOWN OF 1640

By 1640 England was in a state of crisis, a crisis that had been developing since the accession to the throne of Charles I, on the death of his father James I of England and VI of Scotland. As early as 1626 Sir Benjamin Rudyerd had remarked; 'this is the crisis of Parliaments by which we live or die'. There was a breakdown in trust and understanding between Parliament and Charles I that resulted in Charles dismissing Parliament in 1629 and forbidding talk of 'calling another'. This breakdown was the result of several factors.

King Charles I.

Religion

The mainstream of the Protestant state church of England was to a certain extent Puritan – in other words the majority wanted a 'purified' church with a minimum of ceremonies that for them were a leftover from Catholicism. However, Charles and his close adviser William Laud (made Bishop of London in 1628, and Archbishop of Canterbury in 1633), believed in a church whose ceremonies and the 'beauty of holiness' were fundamental. Also, Laud wanted to restore powers to the church that had gradually died out after the Protestant reformation of the sixteenth century.

Many English people were anti-Catholic. Catholics were viewed with suspicion on a political level, as potential allies of England's enemies Spain and France. They were opposed on a religious level because, to Protestants, Catholics were quite simply wrong about the nature of Christianity, indeed had perverted it. Charles and Laud went about systematically changing the ceremonies and services of the Church of England in a way that many thought was part of a secret design to push the Anglican church back towards 'popery'. In addition to Laud's belief in high-church ceremonies, Queen Henrietta Maria was a French Catholic with her own Roman Catholic circle at court, later her own private Catholic chapel. So for many Puritans Charles and Laud were trying to force the Church of England into Catholicism. This aroused the strongest feelings among the group of Puritans of whom Cromwell was one.

Divine right

Charles believed that, in the last resort, he was responsible to God alone for his actions and that kings were God's representatives on earth. He appeared to ride roughshod over the old-established laws and the rights of Parliament, imprisoning those who refused to pay forced loans. By 1628 Parliament had grave concerns that Charles did not understand the spirit of the English constitution. This, combined with their fears about a secret Roman Catholic conspiracy to subvert the Protestant Church of England, led to a final breakdown in 1629 when Charles dismissed Parliament.

Personal rule

The 1630s saw the period of 'personal rule' where Charles ruled without Parliament while Laud tried to move the Church of England towards his idea of a high church, supporting Charles' divine right monarchy. As bishops died, Laud appointed 'Arminian' Laudian prelates who tried to enforce the use of ceremonies, vestments, bowing at the name of Jesus, and the moving of the altar to a railed-in position at the east end of the church instead of a communion 'table' in the centre of the church. These innovations were disliked and distrusted by the more strongly Protestant Puritans as symbolic of the move back to Roman Catholic practices. At the same time, with no parliamentary subsidies, Charles used the royal prerogative to raise money by revising ancient royal rights, including fining gentry who had refused knighthoods. Courtiers were given concessions to exploit trading rights, and patents of monopoly over the sale of products. Charles made the collection of Ship Money, designed to provide a royal fleet in times of emergency, into a permanent tax, which many considered unconstitutional. It seemed as if personal rule was moving towards a Roman Catholic absolutist monarchy in which the religious sensibilities and the legal rights of the subject were doomed.

When Charles attempted to force a Laudian prayer book on his Scottish subjects, who were even more Puritan than their English neighbours, they revolted, signing a National Covenant to resist. Charles could not allow the Scots to rebel and went to war. The war was unpopular with his English subjects, many of whom saw the Scots as fellow sufferers from Laudian church tyranny. The less than impressive English royal army suffered defeat at the hands of the Scots. By 1640 the royal treasury was empty and Charles had no choice but to call a parliament in May 1640 in the hope that it would vote money for a renewed attack on the Scottish rebels. Personal rule had broken down, and a profound crisis in the nation's affairs had begun.

Cromwell's early life

The phrase 'early life' is perhaps a misnomer when dealing with Cromwell. Born on 25 April 1599, he was already 41 in 1640, and still unknown outside his own area. So, for most of his life he was an obscure country gentleman; only in the last eighteen years, between 1640 and his death in 1658, was he a national figure, and this was the result of the crisis in government and the Civil Wars.

Cromwell was born in the small market town of Huntingdon on the edge of the Fen country, which spreads from Peterborough, Cambridgeshire, to King's Lynn, Norfolk, and up into Lincolnshire. He was the son of Robert and Elizabeth Cromwell. His mother was already 34, old by the standards of the time, when she gave birth to Oliver. As the only son to reach maturity, he appears to have revered his mother, taking particular care of her after his father's death. She was 89 when she died in 1654, a great age in the seventeenth century. Oliver's background was that of solid gentry. His mother was from a Norfolk gentry family, the Stewards, while his father was the second son of a quite distinguished line – the Cromwells of Hinchinbrooke. His grandfather Henry had been knighted by Queen Elizabeth and was largely responsible for building the great house there – he entertained lavishly, being called the 'Golden Knight of Hinchinbrooke'. Oliver's father Robert was the Golden Knight's second son. Robert's elder brother Sir Oliver spent great sums on hospitality, in particular on King James I; financial ruin was the result and Hinchinbrooke was sold in 1627. Robert, as the second son, would have had only limited resources and may well have had to supplement these by being a brewer as well as modest landowner.

Many legends have grown up regarding Oliver's early life, including one that, as a baby, he was seized by a pet monkey while on a visit to Hinchinbrooke and carried up on to the roof. An even more unlikely story is that he met the future King Charles when they were both very small and had a fight with him. There is no hard evidence for either of these tales.

He went to Huntingdon Grammar School and this experience may well have had great influence on him. The schoolmaster was Dr Thomas Beard, a quite well-known Puritan who published *The Theatre of God's Judgement* in 1597 and 'a retractive from the Romish religion' in 1616, which he dedicated to Sir Oliver Cromwell. In some ways it was a classical Puritan attack on Roman Catholicism that equated the Pope with the anti-Christ. Like many in the seventeenth century, Beard believed that God's judgements would come upon the wicked in this world as well as the next and that God was ever-present and looking over the shoulders of everyone. It has been argued that Beard's influence shaped Oliver's religious thought and remained one of the mainsprings of his actions. This may be too large a claim. Beard was in some ways a conventional Puritan Calvinist thinker whose ideas were unexceptional in the context of the early seventeenth century, and were commonplace among the more Puritan minded. However, it is interesting that Beard claimed that 'the greatest and mightiest princes are not exempt from punishment' and that 'it is unlawful both by the law of God and man for Kings to tax above measure'. Recent research by **John Morrill** has suggested that in any case Beard was not quite the upright principled man of legend; he seems to have been anxious to further his career and get hold of various lucrative offices.

Also, what little evidence there is tends to the conclusion that the young Cromwell did not follow the strict ideas that Beard tried to inculcate into his pupils. He seems to have been fond of gambling, kissing young women in the street, drinking too much and fighting. He appears to have been fonder of sport than of books even during the year he spent at Sidney Sussex, the Puritan Cambridge college. He did not take a degree because he left the university on the death of his father in 1617. He then spent some time studying law at the Inns of Court in London. There was nothing unusual in a young gentleman spending some time at both university and the Inns of Court without either taking a degree or practising law. Attendance at university and the Inns of Court was part of the education of a landed country gentleman, and most of Oliver's contemporaries would have done the same.

Elizabeth Bourchier.

At the age of 21 he married Elizabeth Bourchier, the daughter of a rich City merchant. Marriage had a stabilising effect on him, and the couple returned to Huntingdon. Elizabeth appears to have been a shrewd, sensible woman who was capable, judging by her letters, of giving Cromwell some gentle advice. Contemporaries found her rather homely and unfashionable. Royalists unkindly called her 'an ape in scarlet'. More neutral observers saw a likeable, if unsophisticated, woman bound up with her husband and her many children. Oliver appears to have been devoted to her, and to their children. Between 1621 and 1629 they had six – Robert, Oliver, Bridget, Richard, Henry and Elizabeth. His youngest daughter Elizabeth was his favourite and he was devastated by her death in 1658.

KEY TERM

Arminianism
Named after the Dutch theologian Arminius, this is the name given to the policies of Archbishop Laud who denied the central Puritan idea of predestination and stressed high-church ceremonies which were associated by many with Roman Catholicism.

In 1628 Cromwell sat in Parliament for Huntingdon. His only speech was one attacking **Arminianism** and he made no real impression nor played any role of importance in the events that culminated in 1629 with the group led by Sir John Eliot holding down the Speaker, passing the Three Propositions, which condemned Charles' tax and religious policies, while refusing to accept Charles' dismissal of Parliament.

However, the years 1628–32 were of great significance in shaping Cromwell's attitudes. He seems to have had some kind of profound personal crisis – almost a nervous breakdown if the fragmentary evidence we have can be relied on. In September 1628 he visited one of the most famous (and rich) doctor-apothecaries in London, Sir Theodore Mayerne, whose fashionable practice included patients from the royal household. He was famous enough to expect patients, however distinguished, to visit him. He was also so fat that he found walking difficult and avoided home visits. He records that Cromwell consulted him because of stomach pains and he found him extremely melancholy. Cromwell's family doctor Simcott said that he would sometimes lie in his bed 'all melancholy', and would also send for Simcott at 'unseasonable hours' such as midnight because he believed he was dying. It must be said that these remarks were made later to a Royalist, Sir Philip Warwick, and cannot be confirmed. It appears that, if there was a mental crisis, it was resolved by a form of religious conversion which Cromwell later referred to in a letter of 1638: 'you know what my manner of life hath been. O I have lived in and loved darkness and hated the light. I was … the chief of sinners … yet God had mercy on me. O the riches of his mercy.'

Some historians have taken this conversion as the turning point in Oliver's life, after which his only motive and ruling passion was 'reformed' Puritan religion. This judgement can be questioned on several counts. Oliver continued to enjoy country pursuits, especially riding and hawking. In the days of his greatness those who wished to find favour with him offered gifts of hawks. He also seems to have enjoyed music and dancing, thus he cannot fit into a stereotype of a strict Puritan. He appears to have developed political skills that argue a very practical attitude to certain problems and situations. That the reformed Puritan religion without an oppressive church organisation came to be one of his main aims is not in doubt, but that it was the only motive force behind his actions is questionable. Another point worthy of mention here is that his conversion did not result in a very narrow view of an elect chosen by God, including himself, that were possessed of the ultimate truth. He seems to have been genuinely concerned for toleration and protection of differing religious views.

As he became more settled mentally and spiritually in the 1630s, so he did he financially. An uncle left him considerable property in Ely and he moved to a house, now a museum, near the cathedral. During his time in Ely he became involved with the question of Fen drainage. The vast flat area of the Fens was still partly a wild landscape and the Fen people made their living by fishing and wildfowling over land that was regarded for all intents and purposes as common land. But there was money to be made from draining the Fens, creating the fertile fields that still are some of the most productive in England. Royal 'patentees' were draining the Fens, depriving the poor of their independent livelihood. Although the details are confused and scanty, it appears that Cromwell supported the rights of the Fen people against the patentees, who included the future Earl of

Cromwell's house in Ely.

Manchester with whom he was to clash spectacularly over another issue in 1644. It seems that Cromwell thought the compensation offered to the common people was not sufficient and he supported them both in 1638 and in Parliament later. This was the origin of the later Royalist nickname 'Lord of the Fens' that Cromwell was given as an insult: Fen people were considered 'rude and uncivil'. He was also fined for refusing a knighthood and was alleged to have been 'a great stickler against Ship Money'. In other words, he formed part of that large section of the gentry who opposed Charles' religious and financial policies in the 1630s.

In 1640 Cromwell represented Cambridge in the Short Parliament, but again did not play a prominent part in its three-week life. With the second defeat of Charles' forces at the hands of the Scots, only the Treaty of Ripon prevented a further Scottish advance. Under the terms of the treaty £850 a day was paid to the Scots, who occupied the six northern counties, and caused a stranglehold on London's coal supply. Economic problems caused Charles to call another parliament which met in November 1640, the Long Parliament. Again Cromwell represented Cambridge.

CONCLUSION

By 1640 England was experiencing a profound crisis, the result of Charles' absolutist policies which were believed to be undermining the old constitution, and his religious policies which were associated with Roman Catholicism. The belief in an absolutist Catholic conspiracy dominated the minds of the gentry coming up to Parliament. In this respect, Cromwell was no different from any other Member of Parliament.

Oliver Cromwell: timeline of events

1599	**April 25th:** Cromwell born in Huntingdon
1616	Enters Sidney Sussex College, Cambridge
1620	Marries Elizabeth Bourchier
1628	MP for Huntingdon
1629-40	Charles I 'Personal Rule'. Cromwell clashes with Royal Patentees over commoners' rights in Fen drainage.
	November: Long Parliament meets. Cromwell MP for Cambridge
1642	First Civil War breaks out. Cromwell raises a troop of horses for Parliament.
1643	Cromwell rises to prominence as a cavalry commander in Lincolnshire for the Eastern Association.
	December: Solemn League and Covenant brings Presbyterian Scots into the War on Parliaments' side.
1644	**July:** Battle of Marston Moor. Cromwell's cavalry are the decisive factor in the defeat of the northern army under Newcastle and Prince Rupert.
	Autumn: Quarrel between Manchester, the Commander of the Eastern Association, and Cromwell who accuses him of not wishing to finally defeat the king.
	Self-denying Ordinance – Parliamentary commanders removed, except Cromwell.
	Winter: New Model Army formed. Fairfax made commander-in-chief; Cromwell becomes commander of the cavalry.
1645	**June:** Battle of Naseby; The king's last field army is defeated. Again, Cromwell's cavalry is decisive.
1646	Last Royalist forces defeated at Langport and Stow-on-the-Wold. The king surrenders to the Scots. Scots hand over Charles to Parliament; The king is held at Holdenby House in Northamptonshire.
	Increasing tension between Parliament and the Army.
1647	**May:** Army rendezvous at Newmarket and agree not to disband until pay demands are met. Independents in the Army oppose any religious settlement that does not include religious toleration.
	June: Army seize the king. Cromwell and Ireton start negotiations with Charles at Hampton Court.
	October: Levellers in the Army hold debates with Cromwell and Ireton at Putney, on the shape of a new constitution. Army occupies London.
	November: Charles escapes from Hampton Court and flees to Carisbrooke Castle on the Isle of Wight.
1648	**Spring:** Second Civil War. Royalist Risings in Kent, Essex, South Wales and Norwich. Scots invade in alliance with Charles.

	August: Battle of Preston; defeat of Scots under Hamilton by Cromwell.
	November: Army decide to try the king. 'Prides Purge' removes majority of MPs unwilling to vote for a trial.
1649	**January 30th**: Execution of Charles I.
	August: Cromwell lands in Ireland.
1650	**June**: Cromwell in Scotland.
	September: Battle of Dunbar. Despite being outnumbered Cromwell defeats the Scots.
1651	Third Civil War. Charles II and Scots invade.
	September: Defeat of Charles II at Worcester. He flees abroad.
1653	**April**: Cromwell dismisses the Rump Parliament.
	July: 'Barebones' or Nominated Parliament meets.
	December: Barebones Parliament surrenders its powers back to Cromwell. Instrument of Government sets up Protectorate.
1654	**September**: First Protectorate Parliament meets, clashes over powers of Protector in the Instrument of Government. Commonwealth's-men withdraw from Parliament.
1655	**January**: First Protectorate Parliament dismissed.
	March: Royalist Rising in the West Country led by Penruddock, put down.
	August: Rule of the major-generals established.
1656	**September**: Second Protectorate Parliament meets. Major-generals rule abandoned.
1657	Moves to offer Cromwell the Crown; he rejects them but accepts the Humble Petition and Advice; he can now name his successor and there is an 'Upper House' established.
1658	**February**: Second Protectorate Parliament dismissed.
	September 3rd: Cromwell dies.

SECTION 2

What was the background to the outbreak of the Civil War?

KEY THEMES

- Between 1640 and 1642 attempts were made to resolve the crisis. They failed because Charles was not firm with his opponents, nor did he attempt to placate them. He did nothing to defuse the belief in an absolutist conspiracy organised by secret Roman Catholics.
- By the end of 1641 some Members of Parliament were determined to put restraints on the king; he was beginning to get some support from more conservative members. The Irish Rebellion made the issue of who controlled the army a crucial one. Charles was not prepared to relinquish this control and his opponents were not prepared to let him have it. This issue led directly to civil war.

THE LONG PARLIAMENT, 1640–2

The men who came up to Parliament in November 1640 were broadly united in what they wanted the Parliament to achieve. They wanted to dismantle the apparatus of 'personal rule' – the royal prerogative courts, the new financial burdens – and stop the moves towards a semi-absolutist state. They wanted to punish or neutralise the king's 'evil advisers', especially Archbishop Laud and Strafford, and they wanted to destroy what they saw as a Roman Catholic conspiracy in Church and State. They were not thinking in terms of civil war at all; they believed that once Charles was freed of his 'evil advisers' he would see his place in a restored, balanced constitution where the subject and the sovereign had their rights.

By the summer of 1641 it seemed as if the Long Parliament had achieved most of its aims. Laud was in prison; Laudian bishops were powerless; the king's most dangerous adviser, the Earl of Strafford, had been executed; and the machinery of personal rule dismantled. However, Charles failed to inspire trust in MPs. His concessions (or surrenders) were reluctant and he left the impression that he would, given the opportunity, reverse the reforms. His French Roman Catholic wife Henrietta Maria and her circle of Catholic courtiers urged him to act decisively against his opponents in Parliament and restore his freedom of action as a divine right monarch.

An engraving of a printed speech by John Pym in 1641.

Master *PYM*

HIS SPEECH

In *Parliament*, on *Wednesday*, the fifth of *January*, 1641,

Concerning the Vote of the House of *Commons*, for his discharge upon the Accusation of High Treason, exhibited against himselfe, and the Lord *Kimbolton*, Mr. *Iohn Hampden*, Sr. *Arthur Hasterig*, Mr: *Strowd*, M. Hollis, by his Majesty,

The true Effigies of Mr. Iohn Pym, Esquire

London Printed for I. W, 1641.

On the other side, the leading Parliamentarian John Pym was unbending in his desire to put further restraints on the king whom he did not trust; so a settlement was not in prospect. Rumours of army plots against Parliament and secret Catholic intrigues increased the tension.

In the summer, Charles was in Scotland to ratify the peace treaty with the Scots. A failed attempt by some extreme Royalists to kill the Scottish covenanter leaders, 'the incident', confirmed Charles' deviousness in the eyes of Parliament (although he may have had no firm knowledge of it). When Parliament reassembled in October 1641 the atmosphere was still one of crisis. However, one group in Parliament took the line that most of Parliament's 'grievances' had been satisfied and that the king had to be trusted if the constitution was to work. For the first time there were two sides in Parliament. Pym, fearing that his control over Parliament was slipping away, introduced the Grand Remonstrance with its reminders of the king's past actions, and its assertion of the existence of a Catholic conspiracy to justify the revolutionary demands that Parliament should choose the king's ministers and control the militia (the armed forces). MPs drew their swords and argued fiercely and the Grand Remonstrance was passed by only eleven votes. It seemed as if the king now had a party in the House of Commons prepared to defend the old constitution.

The crisis worsened when, on 1 November 1641, news broke out that the Roman Catholic native Irish had risen in rebellion against the Protestant settlers of Ulster. Absurd tales of 50,000 Protestants massacred were widely believed; in fact, a total of about 5000 died. This strengthened Pym's argument that there was a Roman Catholic conspiracy in England, and to make matters worse the rebels claimed (falsely) to be acting in Charles' name.

The Irish Rebellion became the trigger for civil war in England, because it turned the theoretical question of command of the army into a practical one. An army would have to be raised to put down the rebellion – could Charles be trusted with control of that army? Pym and his supporters argued not. Charles could, perhaps, have defused the crisis by appointing a commander such as the Puritan Earl of Essex in whom Parliament would have had trust. In the event he failed to nominate a commander.

Then, on 5 January 1642, prompted by Henrietta Maria and her group, Charles made a fatal error. He attempted to arrest five leading members of the 'opposition' in the House of Commons, by entering the Palace of Westminster with 300 armed men. The wanted men – Pym, Holles, Strode, Heselrige and Hampden – had been warned and were safe in the City of London, which had supported Pym for the last six months. This

Charles' attempt to arrest the Five Members, 5 January 1642.

failed military coup was another milestone on the road to war because it seemed to confirm Pym's thesis that the king was in the hands of a dangerous Roman Catholic absolutist clique. Under Pym's influence the London mob became so threatening that Charles left London on 10 January 1642, never to return until a prisoner. Once the king left London civil war became more likely.

'We sink insensibly into this state of civil war' was the comment of the MP Sir Harbottle Grimston, and in some ways he was right. England drifted into a civil war that probably only a few extremists on the Royalist side wanted.

The gentry armed themselves, fearing the country would slide into anarchy as social disorder spread. This disorder resulted from a trade depression and a poor harvest. It was accompanied by an alarming growth in radical preaching and pamphlets were distributed calling for all sorts of religious and political change. At the same time both sides engaged in a propaganda war to persuade the large number of uncommitted to support them. Both the king and Parliament tried to raise forces using legal devices: the Royalist commission of array, a long disused medieval device, called people to arms to support their monarch; Parliament passed the militia ordinance, calling for troops in Parliament's name. The king also tried, unsuccessfully, to seize the arsenals at Hull and Kingston-upon-Thames.

By the summer of 1642, it seemed that Parliament had been more successful in gaining support and Pym felt confident that the king would have to give way. There had been armed clashes but no all-out war. In June 1642, Parliament presented the king with the Nineteen Propositions, a final approach that left little room for compromise. The king would have to give up command of the armed forces; Parliament would choose the king's ministers; Parliament would control Church matters; Parliament would appoint guardians for the king's children. These demands would have made Charles almost a constitutional monarch in the modern sense of the term. It left Charles, a believer in divine right, with no choice. It was abject surrender or fight. Perhaps to Pym's surprise, Charles chose to fight, formally raising his standard at Nottingham on 22 August 1642.

WHAT WAS CROMWELL'S ROLE IN THE EVENTS OF 1640–2?

Cromwell's prominence in the Long Parliament up to 1642 can be exaggerated. He became a dominant figure later, and it is too easy to give him an importance that he did not have. He was a backbencher wholeheartedly supporting Pym's group in its assault on divine right monarchy and the Laudian innovations in the Church. He sat on various committees including one of particular interest to him, enclosures of drained Fen land. Cromwell's role was that of defending commoners' rights. He sat on the committee to consider complaints against Bishop Wren of Ely, one of Laud's strongest supporters. Cromwell also championed the cause of John Lilburne, who later caused him trouble as a Leveller. Lilburne had been whipped and imprisoned for distributing unlicensed pamphlets, including some attacking the bishops. Cromwell saw him as a classic Puritan victim of Laudian oppression and was influential in securing his release. Cromwell up to that time was no more than a reasonably well-known MP and by no means a very significant force in the House of Commons.

However, perhaps some saw more than a badly-dressed country squire whose speeches were passionate but ill-formed. Hampden, a relative of Cromwell, was asked who he was, 'for I see he is of our side, by his speaking so warmly this day'. 'That slovenly fellow which you see before us', replied Hampden, 'who hath no ornament in his speech, I say that sloven if we should come to have a breach with the king (which God forbid) in such case will be one of the greatest men in England.'

Cromwell, of course, supported the Grand Remonstrance, in fact underestimating the conservative reaction that was setting in. When it did pass he remarked to the moderate Royalist Falkland that 'if the Remonstrance had been rejected he would have sold all he had the next morning and never have seen England more, and he knew there were many other honest men of the same resolution'.

As the final breach with the king loomed, Cromwell threw himself into the defence of Parliament. On 14 January 1942 he 'moved that a committee be named ... to put the Kingdom in a posture of defence'. He gave £2000, a huge sum in today's money, for the defence of Ireland. Most of the money raised, in fact, went to arming Parliamentary supporters in England. By July he was raising troops in Cambridge, and in August prevented the Cambridge colleges from sending their gold and silver plate to the king, lining the Great North Road with musketeers. To seize the property of the colleges by force before war had begun was a daring move: Cromwell could have been tried as a highway robber.

While Cromwell was not a very significant member of the Long Parliament during the years leading up to the Civil War (he was not on Charles' 'hit-list' of five members), as war approached he, unlike many MPs, had no doubts about Parliament's cause. He was prepared to go to war wholeheartedly when so many others moved reluctantly and hesitantly into armed conflict.

In 1642 Cromwell saw action as necessary and his contribution to Parliament's cause was assessed by a contemporary as important:

> *a great ... number of the gentry* [in East Anglia and the East Midlands] *were disaffected to the Parliament ... which might have thrown those counties into as much distraction ... as any other part of the land had felt ... if* [they] *had not been curbed and suppressed by that timely care which the Parliament took, and more particularly by the successful services of one gentleman, Master Oliver Cromwell of Huntingdon.*

CONCLUSION

Cromwell had been a relatively minor figure in the events of 1640–2. However, in the build-up to civil war he was one of a minority of Parliamentarians prepared to go to war with determination and enthusiasm for the Parliamentary cause, in contrast to the majority who went into the conflict with trepidation and reluctance.

SECTION 3

Why did Cromwell rise to prominence in the First Civil War?

KEY THEMES

- Cromwell's military career between 1642 and 1646 was a major factor in his rise to prominence.
- He had firm ideas on how the war should be fought. These proved very successful.

CROMWELL'S CAVALRY

Cavalry were often the decisive weapon in seventeenth century battles. Until Cromwell's innovations, a successful cavalry charge ended with the cavalry out of control, charging off the battlefield to kill fugitives or plunder the baggage train. General Monck referred to the Royalist cavalry as a 'rabble of gentility'. Instead, Cromwell trained his cavalry to rein in and await orders after charging rather than pursue the defeated enemy. The Royalist historian Lord Clarendon remarked: 'though the king's troops prevailed in the charge and routed those they charged, they never rallied themselves again in order, nor could be brought to make a second charge again the same day ... whereas Cromwell's troops, if they prevailed, or thought they were beaten and presently routed, rallied again and stood in good order till they received new orders'.

At first, Cromwell's newly-raised cavalry found themselves involved in a series of small-scale actions to defend the territory of the **Eastern Association** against the slowly advancing Duke of Newcastle, and raids southwards from the Royalist stronghold of Newark. Cromwell was also concerned to arrest Royalists in East Anglia and put down a Royalist rising in Yarmouth without bloodshed. He was the natural choice as military governor of Ely. The skirmishes at Grantham, Gainsborough and Winceby were not great victories for Parliament in the context of a national civil war, but during 1643 they made Cromwell's reputation. This was for several reasons:

- Cromwell's cavalry seemed to be the only Parliamentary cavalry that could consistently beat its Royalist opponents.
- Parliamentary newspapers and newsletters needed victories in the uncertain days of 1643 when the Royalists, after the 'draw' of Edgehill

KEY TERM

Eastern Association The East Anglian counties of Norfolk, Suffolk, Essex, Huntingdonshire and Cambridgeshire formed an association to pool resources of men and money.

in November 1642, seemed to have the initiative. Therefore, any Parliamentary victories tended to be written up. Sir William Waller, a modestly successful general in the west, was given the same treatment, being called 'William the Conqueror'.

- The discipline among Cromwell's troops was a welcome contrast to the looting and riotous behaviour of troops in general. As one Parliamentary source commented, 'How happy were it if all the forces were thus disciplined.'
- Cromwell actively recruited and promoted 'godly' men without too much concern for their social background. He wrote 'I had rather have a plain russet-coated captain that knows what he fights for, than that which you call a gentleman and is nothing else.' This was not because of a lack of respect for social standing, rather for practical reasons: 'It may be it provokes some spirits to see such plain men made captains of horse. It had been well that men of honour and birth had entered into these employments, but why do they not appear? Who would have hindered them? But since it was necessary the work must go on, better plain men than none.'

By January 1644, Cromwell was second in command of the Eastern Association army under the **Earl of Manchester**. His Eastern Association cavalry had already earned the nickname 'Ironsides', bestowed on them by Prince Rupert in reluctant admiration of their hardiness in battle. The military situation for Parliament was more favourable than it had been in 1643, because of the **Solemn League and Covenant** which had put Newcastle's northern Royalist army into a vice between the Scots advancing south and the English Parliamentary forces.

On 2 July 1644, after Rupert had joined the Duke of Newcastle's army and raised the Parliamentary siege of York, the battle of Marston Moor – probably the largest battle on English soil – was fought. Rupert and Newcastle were outnumbered by the Scots, the Yorkshire troops of Sir Thomas Fairfax, and the Eastern Association. The sensible decision, put forward by Newcastle, would have been for the Royalists to retreat. Rupert refused this option. He compounded his error by believing that, as evening was coming on, there would be no battle that day. The Parliamentarians, including Cromwell's cavalry, attacked, smashing the Royalist cavalry opposite. For a while, as the battle raged, it seemed as if the Royalists, despite disadvantages of both ground and numbers, might be victorious – only Cromwell's attack had been completely successful. Both Leven, the Scottish commander, and the Earl of Manchester had fled; but Cromwell, after destroying one wing of Royalist cavalry, wheeled round and attacked the other, and resistance collapsed. It was a tribute to the training of his Ironsides to rein in and await orders after a successful charge. Without Cromwell Marston Moor would probably have been a Royalist victory.

The Earl of Manchester 1602–71
He commanded the Eastern Association army and was to fall out with Cromwell over his hesitant attitude to fighting to the finish, throwing away advantages that he had after Marston Moor and the second battle of Newbury in 1644. Manchester was removed from command by the Self-denying Ordinance of 1645. This said that no peer or MP could hold military office.

KEY TERM

Solemn League and Covenant
The agreement that brought the Scottish Presbyterians into the war in exchange for Parliament agreeing to set up a Presbyterian system of church government in England.

Why did Cromwell rise to prominence in the First Civil War?

The result of the battle of Marston Moor was the loss of the north for the king. It should have led to a swift victory over the remaining Royalists, but the opportunity was not taken. The Scots went off to besiege the port of Newcastle; Fairfax engaged in mopping-up operations against individual Royalist strongholds in the north; and Manchester returned to the east. The other Parliamentary commanders, the **Earl of Essex** and **Sir William Waller**, agreed to advance on the king's headquarters at Oxford in a combined operation. However, their rivalry meant they could not co-operate for long: Essex decided to march his army into the Royalist west of England – Lyme Regis was still holding out for Parliament and he wished to relieve the town.

Charles defeated an army led by Sir William Waller at Cropredy Bridge and pursued Essex into Cornwall inflicting a crushing defeat on his army at Lostwithiel. In October another chance to destroy the Royalists was thrown away by Manchester when he failed to pursue them as they retreated after the second battle of Newbury. So, after two years of war there was no end in sight.

POLITICAL DEVELOPMENTS DURING THE WAR

The Parliamentarians were by no means united during this period. While Pym lived, the cracks under the surface remained hidden but, on his death in December 1643, they appeared. Put simply, there was political division between two groups. Those Parliamentarians who had reluctantly seen war as the last resort, the so-called Peace Party, wanted to end it by negotiation. For many of them even a few concessions by the king would be enough. Charles, however, showed no sign of ever negotiating in earnest. The other group, the so-called War Party, were prepared to fight the war energetically, to defeat the king decisively and then to negotiate from a position of strength. This group looked to Cromwell to achieve their aims.

THE ROLE OF RELIGION DURING THE WAR

Another potential split in the Parliamentary ranks was caused by religion. Many MPs were Presbyterians. They wanted, as part of any settlement with the king, a Presbyterian church, which all would be forced to attend: this was the basis of the Solemn League and Covenant with the Scots. A minority were Independents, who inclined to a looser state church with toleration for those who did not wish to attend it. Many Presbyterians feared that religious toleration would lead to political anarchy, because Independency was believed to be popular among the poorer classes: a strong church was regarded as a bulwark of social order.

The Earl of Essex 1591-1646
Commander of the main field army of Parliament, he was rather hesitant in the field although not entirely unsuccessful. He relieved Gloucester in 1643 and fought his way back to London. He did make a very costly mistake in 1644, marching right down to Cornwall where he was defeated at Lostwithiel with the loss of 6000 men as prisoners. He was removed by the Self-denying Ordinance in 1645.

Sir William Waller c.1597-1688
Commander of the Parliamentary forces in the south and west and a competent soldier, he had some victories but was defeated at Roundway Down in July 1643. He was one of those who opposed the creation of the New Model Army.

Cromwell himself was an Independent with a firm belief in religious toleration. He had powerful allies in Parliament, such as Lord Saye and Sele, Oliver St John and Sir Henry Vane.

By 1644, Parliament was by no means united in its war aims, nor agreed on what sort of settlement might follow a Parliamentary victory.

THE QUARREL BETWEEN MANCHESTER AND CROMWELL

Cromwell's style of warfare and his determination to beat the king disturbed Manchester, who was fighting to bring the king to terms and actually seems to have been worried by the completeness of the victory at Marston Moor. Manchester remarked: 'If we beat the king ninety and nine times yet he is king still … but if the king beat us once we shall be hanged and our posterity made slaves.' Cromwell's reply was typical: 'If this be so, why did we take up arms at first? This is against fighting ever hereafter.'

The breach between Cromwell and Manchester reflected the splits within Parliament. Manchester and his Presbyterian Peace Party allies were becoming deeply suspicious of Cromwell, seeing him as a dangerous radical with his policy of promotion by merit rather than birth. Also, his promotion and protection of Independents made it seem as if he were building up the influence of Independents within the army. For Cromwell, contact with Scottish Presbyterian officers at the time of Marston Moor confirmed his fear that Presbyterians would create as intolerant a church as the Laudian Anglican one had been. He had already clashed with Major-General Crawford, Presbyterian commander of Manchester's forces in Lincolnshire, over Crawford's attacks on **Anabaptist** officers, writing to him: 'Sir, the state in choosing men to serve them, takes no notice of their opinions, if they be willing faithfully to serve … that satisfies.' After Marston Moor, Cromwell's distrust of 'narrow' Presbyterians became open. Furthermore, Cromwell was convinced that Manchester had deliberately thrown away the chance to destroy Charles' army after the second battle of Newbury.

KEY TERM

Anabaptists
Baptists believed in adult baptism to be 'born again'. Most mainstream Puritans, both Presbyterians and Independents, viewed them as extremists.

Self-denying Ordinance
The differences between Cromwell and Manchester were aired in a series of bitter exchanges in the Lords and Commons. This broadened into an assault on not only Manchester but Essex too, and a questioning of the whole organisation and conduct of the Parliamentary war effort. Many MPs who had little or no sympathy for Cromwell's religious ideals regarded him as the man who had done most to prevent Parliament's defeat. There was also a feeling that unless commanders and indeed organisations were changed, the war might drag on for years. So, in a

fairly close-run contest the Peace Party was defeated. The majority of MPs voted for a Self-denying Ordinance, proposed in the Commons by Cromwell himself and in the Lords by Lord Saye and Sele.

The Ordinance laid down that no member of either House of Parliament could hold a commission in the army. This was, in essence, a face-saving device to remove Essex and Manchester without charging them with incompetence. In theory, Cromwell should also have given up his post but, in the event, his command was seen as so vital that he was given a temporary dispensation to continue in the army. Cromwell's opponents saw this as a clever, unprincipled piece of scheming by him but, in fact, as one of the prime movers behind the Ordinance he certainly could not be sure that he would be excepted. He took a considerable risk.

The New Model Army

Cromwell's next contribution to the eventual victory of Parliament was his role in the creation of the New Model Army in the winter of 1644. In essence, the problem facing Parliament was that the various armies under the nominal control of the 'Committee of Both Kingdoms' did not co-operate with one another, as was shown after Marston Moor. Localism dogged these armies. Troops tended to become disorientated, or even deserted, when they were marched out of their own areas. It is estimated that over one-third of Essex's army 'went home' after Edgehill; Essex was reduced to suggesting that the troops might return after they had visited their relatives.

Localism affected even the best motivated of troops on both sides. The Cornish trained bands who fought for Charles, and the London trained bands, some of Parliament's steadiest soldiers, could not be persuaded to campaign for long periods outside their home territories. Even an inspiring and competent commander such as Sir William Waller remarked in despair that his soldiers 'had come to their old cry "home, home"'. Over 50 per cent of infantry in the First Civil War were 'pressed men' – conscripts without even the discipline and motivation of the trained bands or Cromwell's cavalry – so the problem is scarcely surprising. The creation of the New Model Army, urged by Cromwell and Waller among others, was designed to overcome the twin problems of divided command and localism.

The three armies of Waller, Essex and Manchester were put together under the command of Sir Thomas Fairfax, who requested that Cromwell be made Lieutenant-General of Horse under him. While the restructuring took place, Cromwell served under Waller who paid tribute to his being prepared always to obey his superior's orders. This casts an interesting light on the previous quarrel between Cromwell and Manchester, with Manchester's insinuations of insubordination. It would

Cromwell fighting at the Battle of Marston Moor in 1644.

seem that Cromwell was perfectly prepared to obey orders and submit to higher authority if he had faith in the general concerned. He seems to have lost faith in Manchester not only for his reluctance to fight, but also for his failings as a leader.

Victory at Naseby

Within a few days of Cromwell's appointment as Lieutenant-General of Horse, the decisive battle of the First Civil War was fought at Naseby, on 14 June 1645. Rupert had sacked Leicester before Naseby; the king's fortunes seemed to be looking up. Indeed, the New Model Army, derided by Royalists as the 'New Noddle', was not expected to win against the Royalists. Local Northamptonshire people even refused food and fodder to the Parliamentary troops, believing after the fall of Leicester that a Royalist victory was certain, despite the fact that the Royalists were outnumbered.

Prince Rupert's cavalry, the Royalist 'shock troops', crashed straight through the Parliamentary left wing, sending two regiments 'clear away to Northampton', but Rupert could not control his cavalry who continued to gallop off the main battlefield until they reached Fairfax's baggage train. Meanwhile, the Royalist infantry were pushing back the Parliamentary infantry. The day might well have gone to the king but for Cromwell and his Ironsides. Having smashed the Royalist left wing, Cromwell's cavalry actually appeared in front of the king who wished to advance with his life guard. The Earl of Carnwarth, a Scot, stopped the king and his life guard charging at the Ironsides, seizing the king's bridle and reputedly saying: 'Will you go upon your death?' Cromwell did not pursue the retreating king but re-formed his troops and charged into the unprotected Royalist infantry. By the time Rupert returned, the battle was practically over, and he could only cover the king's retreat. The king's cause now appeared lost because of the defeat of his main field army. The victory at Naseby was not the New Model Army's – it belonged to the leadership of Fairfax and particularly Cromwell's cavalry. The New Model Army eventually became a formidable, disciplined fighting machine, having cut its teeth on the campaigns, sieges and small battles as the First Civil War fizzled out. Cromwell's report to the Speaker after Naseby reflects his belief that God was on his and Parliament's side: 'Sir, this is none other than the hand of God and to him alone belongs the victory.' A month later Cromwell greeted another crushing Parliamentary victory, at Langport, in the same vein: 'Thus you see what the Lord hath wrought for us.'

CONCLUSION

As the First Civil War progressed, Cromwell's belief that he was 'doing the Lord's work' was strengthened by the series of victories that he helped to create. This was to give him a sense of destiny, of being God's chosen instrument. However, such a sense of religious certainty did not make Cromwell lose his growing political awareness and his ability to act shrewdly both during the war and in the confused events that followed it.

What were the effects of the First Civil War? The years of revolution, 1646–9

KEY THEMES

- The First Civil War had a number of important effects. Developments during the war made the situation in 1646, when Charles finally surrendered to the Scots, far more complex and unstable than during the crisis of 1642.
- In many ways the revolutionary upheavals that ended with Charles' execution in January 1649 were the result of his deliberate policy of preventing a settlement.

INTRODUCTION

Several factors during the First Civil War caused the political upheaval that followed.

The collapse of the authority of the Church of England meant that unorthodox religious views began to spread, especially among the classes below the gentry. The end of censorship caused a great outpouring of pamphlets on both religious and political ideas. By 1645, there were 722 uncensored 'newsbooks'. Although perhaps only one adult in five could read, the pamphlets and newsbooks were read out to the illiterate. The Parliamentary army became a focus for new religious and political ideas. We have seen how the majority of Cromwell's Eastern Association cavalry were Independents. With the creation of a 'national army' in the New Model Army, these ideas spread. The war had the effect that conservative MPs in 1642 had feared, a partial collapse of the traditional gentry rule of the countryside; the gentry were often absent or stripped of local power because they were living in territory controlled by the side they did not support. The law courts even ceased to function regularly.

There was a potential division between the majority in Parliament, who wanted a Presbyterian settlement, and a minority of Independent MPs. The army tended to independency. When the last Royalist field force surrendered at Stow-on-the-Wold, the commander of its infantry, Sir Jacob Astley, made a prophetic remark: 'You have done your work well boys and may go and play, unless you fall out among yourselves.' The assumption was that, once Charles was defeated, he would see the logic of his position and swiftly come to a settlement with Parliament. Charles, aware of the potential splits in the ranks of his opponents, had no intention of coming to a settlement. He negotiated with the Scots, Parliament and later the army; with all of them he spun out negotiations, hoping for an outright quarrel between his enemies, and consequent anarchy. He hoped that, as the traditional symbol of order, he would be returned to his former position of authority.

WHAT WAS CROMWELL'S ROLE IN THE EVENTS OF 1646–9?

In this period, Cromwell emerged as the key figure. To understand his often confusing changes of attitude it is necessary to try to establish what exactly Cromwell's own aims and ideology were.

Cromwell's beliefs

Cromwell as an Independent was concerned that any settlement would include freedom of religion; people should not be forced to attend church services that did not accord with their beliefs. As he once said, he would rather see Mohammedism (Islam) allowed 'amongst us rather than one of God's children persecuted'. Given this attitude of religious toleration, it is not surprising that he found himself opposed to the Presbyterian majority in Parliament who wanted any settlement with the king to include forcible attendance at a Presbyterian state church. He, of course, had no objections to tolerant Presbyterians who would not insist on church attendance.

Cromwell was, in some ways, still a conservative country gentleman. Until 1648 he believed that any settlement would have to include the continuation of monarchy. When he finally decided against monarchy, it was not because of a theoretical political idealism, but because of the conduct of Charles I. Cromwell believed in a balanced constitution with the monarch enjoying his or her rights and the subject having the ancient rights of the common law constitution. In his view, this balance had been upset by Charles' attempt to set up a divine right, Roman Catholic-influenced monarchical dictatorship. Cromwell recognised that Charles had not relinquished his claims, even in 1648. Therefore, be became a republican reluctantly, by experience rather than inclination.

When faced with demands by the radical Levellers within the army for a new constitution that would have been revolutionary in seventeenth-century terms, he did not oppose them because of their political theory, but because he believed that their ideas would lead to anarchy. 'I am not wedded and glued to forms of government', he once remarked. The idea that all adult males should vote was opposed by him on the grounds that, given the dangerous times after the Civil War, such demands would lead to anarchy which he feared more than anything else. While his son-in-law, Henry Ireton, attacked the Leveller proposals of 1647 from the standpoint of a worked-out, coherent political philosophy, Cromwell was worried about the collapse of society: 'How do we know if, whilst we are disputing these things another company of men shall [not] gather together and put out a paper as plausible as this [the Leveller *Agreement of the People*], and not only another, and another but many of this kind? And if so ... would it not be utter confusion?'

Cromwell's style of speech was hesitant and often repetitive, making it hard to judge whether or not he had decided on a course of action, or indeed what he actually thought. Often, he seems to be thinking aloud, or on the spur of the moment, not necessarily weighing his words. On the other hand, he spent a long time in prayer and contemplation – what he called 'waiting on the Lord'. But once his mind was made up, he acted quite swiftly and ruthlessly, all doubt extinguished.

During 1647, Cromwell found himself in a difficult position, as Parliament and its army were increasingly at odds. He had gone to war, partly to support the rights of Parliament against divine right monarchy, and he was in some ways a typical backbench MP. On the other hand, he had played a major part in the creation of the New Model Army, and had led it to a series of remarkable victories. The officers were his comrades in arms and he had a bond with them. By and large, with the exception of some of the more radical Levellers, the army trusted him and looked to him to protect their interests; Parliament seemed to be intent on treating them with almost unbelievable ingratitude. With his fear of anarchy, the nightmare for Cromwell was the army dissolving into factions, each taking the law into its own hands. This could lead to either a total breakdown of law and order, or a Royalist comeback. He was also aware that Denzil Holles and the rest of the conservative Presbyterians in Parliament were his enemies, fearful not only of his influence over the army, but of the **independency** that the army wanted as part of any settlement.

With hindsight it is easy to see Cromwell as a schemer who defeated the Levellers and executed the king as part of a well-laid plan. In the confused years of 1646–9, Cromwell was picking his way, not laying traps for his opponents. We know the end of the story, but he did not. Indeed, in 1647 it was uncertain whether Cromwell could survive the confrontation between a politicised army, a Presbyterian Parliament and a devious, self-righteous king determined to destroy all his former opponents. Both the Royalists, who saw him as plotting the king's death from 1646 onwards, and the Levellers, who felt betrayed by him – 'you shall scarce speak to Cromwell about any thing, but he will lay his hand on his breast, elevate his eyes and call to God to record, he will weep,

KEY THEME

Independency in the army
Independent preachers had infiltrated the army from 1643 onwards. Cromwell himself had promoted Independent officers. The army therefore was composed of more Independents than Presbyterians – a worry for Holles and the Presbyterian majority in the House of Commons.

howl and repent, even while he doth smite you under the first rib' – believed he was calculating. However, Cromwell was not in charge of the events of 1646–9. He was, to a certain extent, carried along by them. We may well find the Levellers' ideas of democracy attractive and modern; to Cromwell they spelt potential anarchy in an illiterate society where the majority of the population was not politically aware. As far as the king was concerned, Cromwell came to see him not as an essential part of an ordered settlement after years of bloodshed, but a man 'against whom God had witnessed' by allowing his defeat, and who was prepared to plunge the country into further chaos and war rather than accept any settlement that did not restore the powers he had wielded before 1642. Both the radicals and the Royalists represented potential anarchy, not stability. The paradox of Cromwell destroying both the monarchy and the 'revolution' can be explained in terms of a desire for peace, toleration and settlement, rather than personal ambition.

Cromwell aligns with the army

In 1647, Parliament had paid off its Scottish allies and secured the king, and was negotiating with him on the basis of a Presbyterian settlement. However, Denzil Holles and his supporters in Parliament became increasingly concerned about independency within the army. They were determined to disband the New Model Army as soon as possible, and build up a reliable militia of Presbyterians under Massey, a conservative whose loyalty to Parliament in 1645 had been suspect. In the event, Holles made a serious error; the army was offered six weeks' pay and disbandment, or service in Ireland under reliable Presbyterian officers. The pay of the infantry was in arrears to the tune of eighteen weeks, and that of the more politically aware cavalry 43 weeks. Some officers petitioned Parliament for their pay, but were threatened with arrest.

Cromwell, back in Parliament, attempted to protect the interests of the army. In May 1647, as discontent welled up in the army, he addressed a meeting of officers at Saffron Walden, Essex, to persuade them to continue to have faith in Parliament; but he must have been taken aback by the strength of feeling against Parliament. On 29 May 1647, the army broke into revolt, despite Cromwell's efforts to bridge the differences. It held a rendezvous at Newmarket, and issued the 'Solemn Engagement', declaring the army would not disband until it had received a settlement that had the approval of a council of the army composed of senior officers, junior officers and soldiers.

Cromwell decided that he must align himself with the army and try to control, as much as possible, this dangerous revolt, for which, given the Commons' vote on army pay, he had a lot of sympathy. He left London for the army on 3 June 1647. He seems to have had little or no knowledge or influence over the early political statements of the army, such as the 'Solemn Engagement'. Indeed, Henry Ireton seems to have been instrumental in these demands for regular parliaments and liberty of conscience. However, Cromwell would not have found much to argue with them. By July, Cromwell and Ireton were working on the Heads of Proposals, with some of Cromwell's Parliamentary allies, such as St John and Lord Saye and Sele. The Heads of Proposals were a sensible way forward, designed as a basis of negotiations with the king, whom the army was now holding, after Cornet Joyce had taken him from Parliamentary custody at Holdenby House in June. Cromwell claimed to know nothing of this bold move by Joyce, a very junior officer, and it is hard to be sure of the truth. However, by holding the king, by issuing a declaration – 'we are no mere mercenary army hired to serve any arbitrary power of a state, but called for ... by the several declarations of Parliament, to the defence of our own and the people's just rights and liberties', by calling for 'corrupt and delinquent' Members of Parliament to set a date for its dissolution, and by formulating the Heads of Proposals, the army had seized the initiative from Parliament. The balance of power had shifted to the army, now trying to reach a constitutional settlement with the king, and Cromwell was a key figure in this.

Cromwell found himself trying to do a balancing act between the minority in Parliament who were his allies, the king, who wanted to spin out negotiations, and the more radical Levellers. These last regarded negotiations with the king with deep suspicion, calling the senior officers 'grandees', implying they were selling out the interests of the common soldiers to reach a settlement which would not change the fundamentals of the constitution. Cromwell was anxious to prevent the radicals in the army forcing a march on London to put pressure on Parliament. But on 26 July a conservative Presbyterian mob, possibly organised by Holles, invaded the House of Commons and invited the king to London. Cromwell's hand was forced and he and Fairfax ordered the army to occupy London.

At this point, it should have become clear to Charles that the only settlement that could be enforced was one made with the senior officers in the army, in particular Ireton and Cromwell, and their Independent allies in Parliament. Only they had the power to enforce a settlement. It is instructive to look at the Heads of Proposals as a guide to Cromwell's thinking at this time. There would be biennial parliaments; constituencies would reflect the varying sizes of populations (that is, counties that had larger populations would have more MPs); Parliament would control the army and navy; and ministers would be appointed by Parliament. There would be a national church with bishops and the Book of Common Prayer, but the bishops would have no powers over lay people and no one would be forced to attend church; Protestants could worship as they wished.

Interestingly, in view of the later portrayal of Charles as a martyr for the Church of England, he did not accept the only settlement offered that allowed the Church of England to continue to exist. He spun out the negotiations at Hampton Court, still hoping for further splits among his opponents. Cromwell and Ireton came to realise that Charles had no intention of negotiating in a meaningful way.

Meanwhile, the radicals in the ranks of the army became increasingly restive. They drew up the Leveller **Agreement of the People** as an alternative to the Heads of Proposals. The pamphlet was debated in Putney church in October 1647, in a remarkable discussion between the senior officers, led by Cromwell and Ireton, and the Leveller representatives.

From the outset of the debates, Cromwell was anxious above all else to maintain the unity of the army. However, there could be no common ground between Ireton's insistence that the right to vote should remain with those who were property holders – who had 'a permanent fixed interest in the Kingdom' – and the assertion of Levellers such as Colonel Rainborough 'that the poorest in England hath a life to lead as the greatest he'. For Ireton, those who had no property could not be trusted to vote responsibly and indeed might even vote to take property away from those who had it. For the Levellers, 'free born Englishmen' had the right to vote. Only democracy was legitimate: 'I think it's clear that every man that is to live under a government ought first by his own consent … put himself under that government', and 'the foundation of all law lies in the people'.

Cromwell's reaction to the debates was to look for compromise, allowing that the franchise might be extended 'somewhat'; he suggested prayer meetings at difficult points. However, the main thrust of his contribution was to point out the danger of anarchy. There was little hope that the spectre of anarchy and the practical compromise could bridge the gap between two fundamentally opposed political philosophies. The debates closed, partly because of the king's escape from Hampton Court on 11 November.

Charles' escape transformed the situation. Some have even suggested that Cromwell connived in it in order to unite the army, or to trap him into making moves that would lead to his death. It seems unlikely, but doubt remains. What is certain is that Leveller agitation was put down at Corkbush, with one trooper executed for refusing orders, and the army united behind Cromwell and Fairfax against the dangerous development that heralded another Civil War.

Agreement of the People This demanded: biennial parliaments; no authority above Parliament; all to be equal in the eyes of the law; parliamentary constituencies to be of the same size in terms of population; all males over 21 to be able to vote.

At Carisbrooke, Charles concluded an alliance with conservative Scottish Presbyterians, agreeing to establish the more extreme Scottish form of Presbyterianism in England for three years in exchange for Scottish military support to establish him in power without other restrictions to his powers, such as those put forward by Parliament. In Parliament, Cromwell made an impassioned speech for the vote of 'No Addresses', that is, there would be no negotiations with the king.

The Second Civil War, summer 1648

This was a much more incoherent affair than the first. Risings took place in Kent, Essex, south Wales and Norwich. They seem to have been directed as much *against* high taxation, the hated Parliamentary County Committees and the army as they were *for* pure undiluted royalism. The risings were not co-ordinated and, despite the apparent danger of the situation, the army put them down without too much difficulty. One feature of the fighting was the increased bitterness many in the army, including Fairfax and Cromwell, felt. They thought that God had witnessed against the Royalist cause and therefore those who took up arms for the king were pushing the country into another civil war not only unnecessarily but also against the will of God. Some Royalist defenders at Colchester, for instance, were shot after the fall of the town. The main threat came from the Duke of Hamilton's Scottish army; after dealing with the Welsh rebels, Cromwell and Major-General Lambert moved quickly north to meet it at Preston on 17 August.

Hamilton had a large force, but he made some fatal errors that contributed to his defeat. However, the judgement and skill of Cromwell cannot be doubted. After a very hard fight, he inspired his troops to go forward and the Scots broke: with their defeat Charles' last hope was gone.

With the end of the Second Civil War, the gap between the conservative and moderate, largely Presbyterian majority in Parliament on the one hand, and a minority of Independent MPs and the army on the other, widened again. For the majority of MPs there could be no settlement without the king and the vote of 'No Addresses', to Cromwell's fury, was repealed on 17 August 1648. Parliament started to negotiate with the king at Newport. The attitude of the army had been foreshadowed at the Windsor prayer meeting before the army marched off to fight the Second Civil War. At this meeting it was agreed 'that it was our duty, if ever the Lord brought us back again in peace, to call Charles Stuart, that man of blood, to account for that blood he had shed'.

THE TRIAL AND EXECUTION OF THE KING

Cromwell was, at first, not the prime mover in the events that followed. Although he eventually came to see the justice and necessity of the king's execution, he appears to have wavered a little from the attitudes reported at the Windsor prayer meeting. While Ireton and the army had decided on a trial and carried out **Pride's Purge** to keep out MPs who would never vote for a trial of the king, Cromwell was still conducting the siege of Pontefract, where a few Royalists were holding out. He did not arrive in London until after the purge.

In a letter written before the purge to Robin Hammond, the commander of Carisbrooke Castle, Cromwell attacked the treaty of Newport and called Charles 'this man against whom the Lord hath witnessed'; and he expressed satisfaction with Pride's Purge. On the other hand, there is some evidence that, when faced with the awful prospect of the king's execution, he wavered, if only momentarily. The rejection of any compromise was, according to one source, phrased: 'when it was first moved in the House of Commons to proceed capitally against the king, Cromwell stood up and told them, that if any man moved this upon design, he should think him the greatest traitor in the world, but since providence and necessity had cast them upon it, he should pray God to bless their councils'. Another version of the speech is: 'Since the providence of God hath cast this upon us, I cannot but submit to providence.' The second version ties in with the often quoted, alleged remark of Cromwell – that the trial and execution were a 'cruel necessity'.

As usual, once Cromwell had made up his mind he was determined. He told Algernon Sidney: 'We will cut off his head with the crown on it.' In the event, after a trial during which the king refused to plead or speak, on the perfectly legal grounds that there was no court in England that could try him, 59 members of the 'High Court of Justice' set up by the Rump signed the death warrant. After the restoration, some of the regicides, including Richard Ingoldsby, who had performed a deft change of sides in 1660, claimed that Cromwell had forced them to sign. There is absolutely no independent evidence that this happened, and Lucy Hutchinson – whose husband was a regicide, but had no love for Cromwell – specifically denied the story. Cromwell had been a leading figure in the trial and execution, but he had not acted alone and he had the support of the army. However, the execution of the king was carried out by a small minority of the political nation in the belief that there would be no settlement while the king lived and that he was in modern terms a 'war criminal'. It solved an immediate problem but became a legacy that haunted succeeding regimes; for most people, whatever their views about Charles' conduct, the execution of an anointed sovereign was a terrible, unthinkable act, and Cromwell was one of those most associated with it.

The execution of Charles I, 30 January 1649.

CONCLUSION

Why then had Cromwell risen from comparative obscurity to being a key figure by the time of the establishment of the republic? The reasons for Cromwell's rise are almost entirely military. He was not wealthy; he was not an elegant speaker in the Long Parliament; and he seemed the classic Puritan backbencher. His religious views were more strongly Puritan than most; Independents were a minority, however significant, in a largely Presbyterian House of Commons. His rise was due to his military abilities. By 1644 he was the one soldier that Parliament could not do without: he never lost a significant battle and he created the formidable Eastern Association cavalry. His 'political' base was also in the army. His policy of promotion by merit and the advancement of Independents gave him a powerful following of people who owed their careers to him and who trusted him to look after their interests. Thus, on the one hand, he was able to withstand attacks on him by Peace Party Presbyterians while the war lasted, discrediting Essex and Manchester because he could win battles; on the other hand, he was able to neutralise the effects of the Leveller-inspired agitation because, in the last resort, the soldiers trusted him rather than theoretical political idealists, such as John Lilburne and

Colonel Rainborough. Despite some dangerous moments his control over the army was secure and that control gave him enormous potential power. No other officer, not even the popular Fairfax, could control the army. No government in England could survive without army support and the army was Cromwell's – its victories, its officers were his creation.

SECTION 5

Why had Cromwell become Lord Protector by 1653?

KEY THEMES

- Between 1649 and 1653 Cromwell became the arbiter of English affairs. This happened despite the fact that military campaigns took him away from politics at first.
- Although the Leveller agitation had been suppressed, the army still hoped for reforms from the new republic. As it became increasingly obvious that the Rump was not prepared for the reforms that the army wanted, tensions grew.
- By 1653 Cromwell found himself having to choose between the army and an increasingly unpopular Rump, some of whose members distrusted him personally.

THE RUMP PARLIAMENT AND ITS PROBLEMS

The republican government of the Rump Parliament was established during 1649. The monarchy and the House of Lords were abolished; a Council of State and the Rump ruled England. Cromwell was the leading member of the Council of State but, as commander in chief of the army (after Fairfax's resignation in 1650), he did not take a great part in the day-to-day running of the country.

The Rump had considerable problems. The years 1649 and 1650 were marked by poor harvests and the Civil Wars had left huge public debts, so high taxation was inevitable. Military expenditure because of the wars in Scotland and Ireland, and later with the Dutch, was also a major cause of high taxation. There were also possible threats from Spain and France. Politically, the Rump faced opposition from conservatives, who saw it as an illegitimate regicide regime, and from radicals, who hoped that the execution of the king would be the start of political and social reforms. Most Rumpers were not in favour of political or social reforms; even the convinced republicans among them, such as Sir Arthur Heselrige, Thomas Scot and Sir Henry Vane, did not want sweeping changes. It was enough to have set up a 'conservative' republic of property holders. Many Rumpers had only accepted the execution of the king as a last resort; they were not even republicans in the true sense of the word. The Rump needed the support of the army if it was to survive at all. And yet the army always wanted to push it in the direction of reform of the law and social justice, which would have made it even more unacceptable to the conservative country gentry. The Rump appeared to be in a very difficult position.

War in Ireland

The Rump was faced most immediately with war in Ireland, where Royalists were holding out in an uneasy alliance with the Roman Catholic rebels of 1641. In August 1649, Cromwell arrived in Ireland to put down the rebellion. His task was made easier by division among the Irish themselves and by a victory over one of the most dangerous Royalists, Ormonde, who was defeated before Cromwell arrived. Cromwell's campaign in Ireland, which resulted in complete victory, has gone down in history as a particularly brutal one, with massacres at Drogheda and Wexford. New research, however, has cast doubt on the bloody legend of his Irish campaign (see Section 8).

Charles II and the Scottish Presbyterians

Meanwhile, a much more dangerous threat to the existence of the Rump emerged in Scotland, as Charles II, proclaimed in Scotland, made an agreement with the Scottish Presbyterians after their defeat of the charismatic Marquis Montrose. Fairfax refused to fight against his former allies, the Scots, so Cromwell became commander in chief. It is alleged that Cromwell plotted to obtain the supreme command by ousting Fairfax, but Lucy Hutchinson wrote: 'To speak the truth of Cromwell, whereas many said he undermined Fairfax, it was false; for in Colonel Hutchinson's presence, he most effectually opportuned him to keep his commission, lest it should discourage the army and the people at that juncture of time, but could by no means prevail.' Subsequently, in September 1650, Cromwell smashed a vastly superior Royalist army at Dunbar. The very competent General Lambert led the army, and gradually the rest of Scotland fell to the English republicans. In some ways this was only a respite because, in the summer of 1651, Charles II headed another invasion of England, only to be crushingly defeated by Cromwell at the 'crowning mercy' of the battle of Worcester on 3 September. Cromwell had made the new republic secure from Royalist military threats and his influence was now at its height.

The Levellers

Cromwell's first priority after the execution of the king was to restore stability by appealing to the more conservative Parliamentarians who had been shocked by the execution and who feared social upheaval. Therefore, he stamped down on the Levellers, who he saw as a threat to order in a period of traumatic upheaval. His fear of anarchy made him see the Levellers, with whom he had previously negotiated, as dangerous. Lilburne, the Leveller leader, alleged he heard Cromwell say to the

Council of State: 'I tell you, you have no other way to deal with these men but to break them, or they will break you.' Cromwell put down a Leveller mutiny in the army at Burford, and the conservative nature of the regime soon dashed the hope of Levellers who thought the execution of the king would lead to political changes on the lines of the Agreement of the People. Lilburne's disillusion with the republic found its voice in his pamphlet *England's New Chains Discovered*. At this stage, Cromwell was trying to appeal to the traditional political nation. He attempted to prevent the House of Lords being abolished, and encouraged some MPs who had opposed Pride's Purge and the execution to take their seats in the Rump Parliament.

In conversation with the Rumper Bulstrode Whitelocke Cromwell allegedly expressed some support for a monarchical government. 'What', he asked, 'if a man were to take it on himself to be king?' One must, however, view some of these utterances with caution. Cromwell often thought aloud, almost in a 'stream of consciousness', without coming to a conclusion and often in a contradictory manner. What is fairly certain is that between 1649 and early 1652 he was conservatively minded, trying to woo the traditional political nation. However, as time went on other influences and sides to his nature emerged. Without supporting the Leveller position, he began to look for modest reform from the Rump. He looked in vain. The Rump was reluctant to consider law reform and religious toleration, two aims that Cromwell held dear. The Hale Commission on law reform was set up after pressure from Cromwell, but none of its recommendations were acted upon, partly because of the vested interest of the large number of lawyer MPs in the Rump. Concerning religion, the Rumpers were scared of the new religious sects with their unconventional ideas: compulsory church attendance was voted down only by the casting vote of the Speaker, while a blasphemy act was passed. The Rump's idea of religious toleration was a narrow one.

The army

At the same time, the army, although no longer in any significant way Leveller influenced, shared the vague hopes of reform that the Rump was failing to deliver. To the senior officers, the leading Rumpers, such as Heselrige and Scot, seemed to be self-serving oligarchs, now content to have established a 'conservative' republic of the property holders. More importantly, they appeared to be hostile to the army. This hostility was based on the expense of keeping the huge standing army of over 50,000 men. Furthermore, Rumpers were suspicious that the army's senior officers still looked to the Heads of Proposals, with the plans for biennial parliament, which would mean fresh elections. To the army, the Rump was a disappointment; it seemed to be ungrateful considering that the army had made the Rump's position secure by its victories. On the other hand, the unfortunate Rump was in an impossible position: it could not be radical to please the army and at the same time popular with the traditional political nation. One of the main reasons for the Rump's unpopularity with the public was the high taxation, taxation that went to pay the very army that was beginning to distrust it.

CROMWELL'S POSITION

As the army and the Rump drifted apart Cromwell, who had sympathy with both sides, was forced to choose between them. He sided with the army, but tried to keep tension between the Rump and the army to a minimum; for example, by trying to dissuade the officers from petitioning for elections.

Cromwell was a shrewd politician who realised that his only secure power base was the army. In the last analysis the army would follow him, but he had no large group of civilian MPs to support him. Furthermore, if he did not lead or guide the army, then ambitious army politicians would seize control; either anarchy or a military coup would follow. He did support the army's leaning towards a version of the Heads of Proposals as offering the best constitutional way forward. His experiences of the last few years, when he had led the army to victory over all his opponents, combined with his deep religious convictions, made him believe that he and the army were God's chosen instruments. Just as God had witnessed against Charles I, God had shown divine favour to him and his army. Although not in a state of religious fervour by early 1653 he was influenced in his belief in some kind of a divine mission by Major-General Thomas Harrison, the Fifth Monarchist.

The senior officers themselves appear to have been divided at this stage, between 'politiques' who saw the future in terms of a new constitutional settlement, and a small group of religious radicals who looked to Harrison, and whose vision of the future was England as the new Jerusalem. Given Cromwell's belief in the English as God's chosen people, and his own soul-searching, he seems to have leaned towards Harrison without sharing all his radical vision. Perhaps also, he had fought in three civil wars, tens of thousands had died, the king had been executed – and all so that Sir Arthur Heselrige and his supporters – a narrow oligarchy of self-interested, often corrupt politicians – could be in power.

Whatever the motives and politics behind opposition to the Rump, with Cromwell and the army opposed to it, its time was running out. The last straw may have been Heselrige's attempt to remove Cromwell as commander in chief. On 20 May 1653, while the Rump were debating a bill for new elections, Cromwell listened, then denounced the Rumpers and, significantly, called in troops of Harrison's regiment to force a

Cromwell dismissing the Rump, 20 April 1653.

dissolution. The exact arguments in the debate are not known. It is possible that the Rump was going to hold genuine elections, but it might also have filled only vacant seats with 'recruiter' MPs, who would have been approved by the present sitting Rumpers, and the present incumbents would hold their seats. Whatever the truth, the dismissal of the Rump showed that not only was the army the arbiter of the fate of the country, but that the real power lay with Cromwell. Before this, whatever his political manoeuvres, Cromwell had been the servant of others; now he was the supreme figure in English politics with the capacity, should he wish, to become a military dictator.

THE BAREBONES PARLIAMENT OR LITTLE PARLIAMENT/NOMINATED PARLIAMENT

It may be that the dismissal of the Rump was an impulsive action by Cromwell, and that he had no clear idea of what sort of settlement would take place. He said to the Rumpers: 'you have sat here long enough, in the name of God go'. There seems to have been little mourning for its demise in the country at large, but there was also no love for the army. Cromwell and the army politicians found themselves in a dilemma. 'Free' elections, where any candidates could stand, might produce a Royalist reaction. Yet even the senior officers baulked at the prospect of a military government. Many of them had a 'reformed' Parliament as set out in the Heads of Proposals as an ultimate aim; like Cromwell, they saw the dismissal of the Rump as an emergency measure. 'I must tell you again, it is only suspended, tis a sword taken out of a madman's hand, till he recover his senses', was the justification of a pamphlet in May.

With aggrieved Rumpers, excluded members from Pride's Purge and Royalists all against them this was not the moment for free elections; hence the nominated assembly or **Barebones Parliament**. In May 1653, 140 members were chosen as a temporary government by the Council of Officers; they immediately called themselves a parliament. Clarendon, the Royalist, called it 'a pack of senseless fellows chosen for their gifts in praying and preaching', but actually the radicals were in the minority. The majority in the Nominated Parliament were minor country gentry; they were politically inexperienced because none had sat in Parliament before.

Perhaps seeing the assembly as a representation of the godly, Cromwell had high hopes, as shown in his speech of 4 July 1653:

> *This scripture I shall remember to you which hath been much on my spirit, Hosea 11th and 12th verse: 'Yet Judah ruleth with God and is fruitful amongst the Saints', it is said before, 'Ephraim did compass God about with lies and Israel with deceit' … Why truly you are called by God to rule with him and for him, and you are called to be faithful with the saints.*

Cromwell was soon disillusioned with the Nominated Parliament because some of its leading members seemed to be intent on tearing up the fabric of society, and terrifying the traditional political nation. Once again his conservative instinct prevailed as members proposed radical measures: for example, reform of the common law along the lines of the law of Moses; the abolition of tithes, thus leaving the clergy without a source of income; and the abolition of the Court of Chancery. Ironically, Cromwell also began to see some members as just as intolerant as the Presbyterians: they wanted to continue the war on the Dutch, and they attacked 'conservatives' in religion. The Nominated Parliament did, however, institute some sensible reforms, such as civil marriage and compulsory registration of birth, marriages and death. Yet, by December 1653, the conservatives in the Nominated Parliament, the 'politique' army officers and Cromwell himself, were seriously alarmed that anarchy would result if it continued – 'the confusion of all things' as Cromwell recalled a year later. Major-General Lambert had been working on a new constitution for some time, anticipating the collapse of the 'godly' experiment with which he had absolutely no sympathy. Therefore, while the religious radicals were holding a prayer meeting on 12 December, the moderates turned up in force and voted the Parliament out of existence. Speaker Francis Rous went to Cromwell and resigned; it appears that there was already a prepared position. Cromwell said later that he knew 'not a tittle' of the resignation until it happened. This seems inconceivable; the senior officers had meetings not only with Cromwell, but also with moderates in the Nominated Parliament before the resignation. The defeat of the religious radicals left Cromwell again as the most powerful man in the country but, unlike in May 1653, now there was a constitution prepared – a constitution that gave him legal powers.

CROMWELL AS LORD PROTECTOR

The Instrument of Government established Cromwell as Lord Protector – almost as a constitutional monarch. Indeed, the first draft referred to Cromwell as a monarch, but he refused the title absolutely. Under the Instrument of Government:

- The Lord Protector was head of state, in control of the army with the consent of Parliament.
- A council was named but there was a system of replacing councillors in which Parliament played a part.
- Religious toleration was established for all, except Anglicans and Catholics.
- There was an annual revenue to pay for a standing army of 30,000 and the navy.
- Every male over 21 with either lands or goods worth £200 or more could vote.

This was the first written constitution that England or indeed Britain ever had. It was a very reasonable attempt to produce a settlement. It remained to be seen whether it would be accepted by a divided political nation.

CONCLUSION

Cromwell had become Lord Protector because he was the only possible choice. He could control the army, to some extent the real power in the land, because of his unique career with it. He had created it, promoted its officers, and led it to a remarkable series of victories. He also sympathised with many of its aims and aspirations. In the last resort, the army trusted him and would follow him even if it meant abandoning the Levellers, or the religious radicals, like Harrison. Unlike most of his officers, he was no 'career' soldier. He was a typical country gentleman of his times, concerned for law and order and stability. So, for some of the gentry who distrusted the army, he was seen as a man who could control it and restrain its more radical elements. He might have been the man who was the driving force behind the execution of the king but, however much he was disliked, he was at least a brake on the 'wild men' of the politicised army. No one else could have provided this unique balancing act and without him the country would probably have descended into chaos. Cromwell was successful through a mixture of military triumph and political shrewdness, seizing his opportunities and avoiding pitfalls made by his enemies; but in the end it was his control of the army that counted.

SECTION 6

How successful was Cromwell in creating a settlement between 1653 and 1657?

KEY THEMES

- Any settlement in the 1650s would be difficult to achieve because of the events of 1642–53 which had created such an unstable situation.
- There were fundamental divisions in the 'political nation'.

DIVIDED POLITICAL NATION

The traditional 'political nation' that had gone to war in 1642 was divided. The country gentry had gone to war either to support the king as a symbol of the existing order, or to oppose him as an innovator who was destroying the old constitution. By 1653, they were divided into several groups:

- Hard-line Royalists would not accept any settlement that did not mean the restoration of power to Charles II.
- Conservative Presbyterians were outraged by Pride's Purge and the execution of the king. Their ideal was the restoration of Charles II, but on terms. These two groups could not co-operate with each other because the Royalists blamed the Parliamentarian Presbyterians for starting a war with Charles I in the first place.
- Conservative republicans, who as Rumpers approved the execution of the king, saw no reason to support any other political, religious or social changes. To have created a republic was enough. To those excluded by Pride's Purge and to hard-line Royalists, these republicans were traitors – to monarchy and to the rights of Parliament.

In addition, the actual size of the 'political nation' had grown to include many who had not taken any part in politics before 1640. These, many from lower social strata than the gentry, had been radicalised by the war and its aftermath.

The divisions were made more complex by the existence of more radical groups. The Levellers, who looked for an extension of the franchise, and the tiny group of Diggers who believed in a form of agrarian communism, fuelled all the fears of the traditional gentry that chaos or social revolution could occur. In fact, after 1650 their influence waned, but some of the junior officers in the army still looked back to the heady days of 1647 and hoped for radical reforms. Perhaps just as important in terms not of numbers, but in the fear they engendered, were the radical religious sects that sprang up during and after the Civil Wars, partly as a result of unauthorised preaching. The Fifth Monarchists were probably the most important group until the end of 1653. This was partly because they had a powerful patron in the army – Major-General Harrison. With the fall of the Barebones Parliament, they became marginalised. The fastest growing sect was the Quakers, who denied all civil authority and seemed to be subversive of both the social and political order. There were other radical sects, such as the Ranters, whose conduct and moral attitudes alarmed Anglicans, Presbyterians and Independents alike. These latter agreed little in religious matters but all saw Fifth Monarchists, Quakers and Ranters as a dangerous menace to political and social order. The sects were seen as blasphemous and completely subversive of all authority.

Of the new forces in English politics, the army was, of course, the most significant. By 1653 it was a professional army – a most important point. It had become a 'vested interest'. Officers who in civilian life had no prospect of advancement beyond the higher ranks of tradesmen or yeoman farmers now had status and a career. They would oppose any attempt to take away their livelihood, which would happen if the army were disbanded. The fatal paradox of republican governments of the 1650s was that they could not survive without the support of the army, yet the cost of the army in taxation was such that no government could be popular. By 1653, there was a deficit of £700,000 due to the cost of the army and navy, and little prospect of lowering rates of taxation that were far higher than those imposed by Charles I. The army also had political aims. Its senior officers wanted a permanent place for the army in the constitution; some junior officers still wanted radical political reforms; others held radical religious views. There was, then, a potential split between the officers themselves, but this did not become apparent in any serious way until late in the 1650s.

Thus, from the beginning of his time as Lord Protector, Cromwell ruled over a nation divided by politics and by religion; a nation potentially far more unstable than the England even of 1642. Outright opposition to the Protectorate came, predictably, from the die-hard Royalists, disappointed Levellers, religious radicals 'on the fringe', the Fifth Monarchists now seeing Cromwell as the 'little horn of the great beast' of Revelations, and the 'Commonwealth's-men' of the dismissed Rump – Heselrige, Scot, Vane and their allies.

Despite the quite bizarre and desperate attempts by the Levellers to build links to Royalist conspirators, the opponents of the Protectorate were so hopelessly divided that they did not pose any immediate threat. However, outside the army and its few civilian political allies, there was little active support either. Grudging acceptance of yet another bewildering change was probably the attitude of most. The Protectorate, at this stage, was underpinned by 'negative' support – fear of another civil war, dislike of the Commonwealth's-men and the desire to avoid the country slipping into anarchy. Goethe wrote: 'when chaos threatens men seek order rather than justice'. The Protectorate might not have been a legal government as far as many of the gentry were concerned, but it was a de facto government, preventing chaos.

PROBLEMS IN THE PROTECTORATE PARLIAMENT

Could Cromwell, supported by the Instrument of Government, provide a settlement that would put down roots in this complex situation? Cromwell was well served by a professionalised civil service, one of the key figures being Secretary John Thurloe. He was a highly efficient man of business who ran a network of informers and correspondents, making sure that the government was well aware of potential dissidents and plots. Thurloe was one of the men behind the scenes that helped make the Protectorate work. His response to the Instrument was positive. He wrote to Bulstrode Whitelocke: 'this change … hath a very general acceptance, especially among the lawyers, the ministers and the merchants who conceived themselves most in danger from the temper of the last Parliament'. In other words, the establishment of the Protectorate had prevented anarchy. Others, such as the republican Ludlow, saw it as Cromwell's betrayal of the 'good old cause' of republicanism for his own ambitious ends, 'like a false hypocrite'.

The composition of the Council of State seemed to reflect Cromwell's desire to placate and reassure the traditional political nation, at the expense of the radicals and republicans. The military were not in a majority on the Council. Most members were from gentry families, however minor; there were three baronets and three members of leading gentry families, who were ennobled after 1660.

When, however, the first Protectorate Parliament opened on 4 September 1654, the 'healing and settling' which Cromwell aimed at soon proved an illusion. From the beginning, the Instrument of Government was criticised. At first, some of the leading figures in the attack were republican Commonwealth's-men such as Heselrige and Scot, who wanted government by Parliament only (that is, without a single person as head of state). By 12 September, attacks on the Instrument had become the issue that dominated the session. Cromwell, perhaps personally aggrieved by these attacks, forced MPs to sign a 'Recognition' that they accepted government by a single person and Parliament. Speaking on that day he at first tried to justify himself from the charge of personal ambition: 'I called not myself to this place. I say again, I called not myself to this place, as God is my witness.' He gave an account of the events of

1653 that had led to the Protectorate, making the point that he had not become a dictator. He then laid down four 'fundamentals' of the Instrument of Government that were not for negotiation:

- government by a single person and Parliament
- Parliaments to be elected frequently and not sit permanently
- liberty of conscience
- control of the armed forces shared by Protector and Parliament.

More than 100 members refused to sign the 'Recognition' and withdrew from Parliament. With the disappearance of the Commonwealth's-men, the problem should have been resolved. However, it was not in Cromwell's nature to interfere or guide MPs, 'to manage' Parliament.

Many MPs, typical country gentlemen, loathed the army and were terrified that liberty of conscience would lead to anarchy. Parliament refused to pay for the army of 50,000 and wanted it cut down to the 30,000 laid down in the Instrument. Ideally, of course, many would have wished it much smaller than that. They also wanted control of the army to pass to Parliament in the event of the Protector's death. There were calls for the monthly assessment that paid for the army to be reduced from £90,000 to £30,000; a compromise was made at £60,000, but it was a grudging one. Attacks were made on liberty of conscience. The City of London, with its strong Presbyterian element, presented a petition for religious uniformity. Parliament imprisoned John Biddle, who had argued against the divinity of Christ. Cromwell had no sympathy for Biddle but was concerned that pressure for religious uniformity would mean attacks on Baptists and even Independents.

The main issue, however, was the deep-seated distrust of the army shown by so many MPs. Yet there was no prospect of cutting down the army as drastically as Parliamentarians wished because any such move would probably have led to an army revolt, which even Cromwell could not have hoped to control. Throughout the 1650s, he reduced the size of the army, purging it of unreliable radical officers, but it was a slow process, done piecemeal. A sudden slashing of its numbers was simply not practical politics. In these circumstances Cromwell dismissed his first Parliament after five short lunar rather than calendar months – the shortest period a parliament could sit under the Instrument.

THE RULE OF THE MAJOR-GENERALS

Early in 1655 a Royalist rebellion broke out in the West Country – Penruddock's Rising. Royalist conspiracy in the 1650s was feeble and inept: most Royalist gentry were unwilling to take up arms again, content for the most part with talk not action. But the Cromwellian government saw reason to fear such conspiracy. When the badly organised Penruddock's Rising broke out in Wiltshire in March 1655, it seemed to be the tip of an iceberg. In the event, the ruthless and brash Major-General Desborough put it down easily: only 400 rebels turned out for Penruddock, other suspected conspirators having already been arrested.

Penruddock's Rising provided one of the reasons to introduce the major-generals' experiment, an episode that helped to create the legend of Cromwell as a military dictator. The rule of the major-generals has tarnished his reputation in the popular mind until the present day: 'the most intolerable experience England ever had', as one of Cromwell's biographers put it. England was divided into eleven districts, each ruled by a major-general. Included in their orders were instructions to collect a 10 per cent decimation tax on Royalist estates.

The major-generals were to set up a new, reliable militia trained by professional soldiers, the cost of the scheme to be met by the decimation tax. The local militia, officered by professional soldiers, would provide employment for officers whom it would otherwise be difficult to dismiss from the army. It opened the way for reducing the numbers in the regular army: rank-and-file soldiers could be dismissed and they would be unable to organise themselves effectively to resist their dismissal. In this way, the standing regular army could be reduced without political upheaval and, most importantly, taxation could be reduced. This might make the regime more popular and would certainly reduce its debt. The major-generals were to:

- seek out 'thieves, robbers and highwaymen'
- suppress horse racing, cock fighting, bear baiting and stage plays, on the grounds that 'treason and rebellion are usually hatched and contrived against the state on such occasions'
- ensure that the Poor Laws were put into effect
- investigate murders, affrays and other crimes
- suppress gaming houses and brothels
- oversee the licensing of alehouses
- keep known Royalists under surveillance and stamp down on any possible conspiracies.

It was hoped that the major-generals would improve public morality. In practice, they varied a great deal in their priorities after the collection of the decimation tax and the setting up of the new militia. Even the collection of the tax was not straightforward – individual Royalists appealed for exemption directly to Cromwell. The tax threshold itself was too high; it was levied on estates worth more than £100 per annum; evasion was common; and the money collected did not cover the cost of the scheme. The tax and militia aside, it seems difficult to see any consistency between the major-generals. Some, such as Desborough, Skippon and Boteler, came down hard on Quakers, seeing them as potentially subversive enemies of the state. Lambert, however, was completely indifferent to them.

Their attitude to the local justices of the peace (JPs), whose co-operation was needed, varied. John Desborough, Berry, Whalley and Goffe seemed to make efforts to get on with them. Others, such as Boteler and Kelsey, rode roughshod over them. Some actually interfered with local privileges and charters; for example, Haynes in Norfolk tried to purge the Norwich City Corporation in order to replace it with Independents. The Council in London, interestingly, ignored his recommendations. Even on the question of public morality they were divided: some closed down large numbers of alehouses, others were indifferent to their existence. On the specific instruction regarding race meetings there was no consistency. Worsley (the most hard-working major-general who actually died from exhaustion) banned them; Whalley permitted them.

The career of Major-General Boteler (or Butler), in charge of Bedfordshire, Northamptonshire and Rutland, demonstrates their worst side, and why they aroused so much resentment. Boteler was a local in the sense that he had been born in Oundle, Northamptonshire and was the son of a butcher and grazier. The classic Cromwellian professional soldier who had carved out a career in the army, he was a Baptist, probably a protégé of Cromwell's son-in-law, the commander of the army, Charles Fleetwood. Boteler used his new position to impress the local gentry by building one of the largest and most important 'Puritan classical' houses still standing, Cobthorne in the centre of Oundle. He was asserting in a tangible way his new powers and status over his former 'betters'. He appears to have run a 'protection racket' against local Royalists in order to finance his building schemes. He even tried to overawe the electors in an unholy partnership with a member of the Council, Sir Gilbert Pickering. His contribution to the 'reformation of manners' was to lock up Quakers. He narrowly escaped impeachment in the Second Protectorate Parliament.

Hostility to the major-generals

Of course, Boteler was probably unusual, but the rule of the major-generals did considerable damage to Cromwell's hopes of 'healing and settling'. Cromwell himself seems to have considered them as agents to push forward his vision of a godly, ordered society. The gentry saw them otherwise. Some of the major-generals were courted by the gentry and they reported that the traditional rulers of the countryside had received them favourably, but that cannot be taken as evidence that they were welcomed. Certainly, the attacks on them in the Second Protectorate Parliament show that they were far from welcomed in the localities.

The hostility was based on several factors. They were mainly seen as low born. Clarendon referred to them as 'tinkers and button makers'. The gentry did not take kindly to being ordered around by their social inferiors. The decimation tax, which fell on Royalists, defined them as those who had been 'in arms' against Parliament from 1642. This opened old wounds that many at a local level were anxious to leave to heal. The institution of the major-generals was an attack on one of the most powerful ideas of the seventeenth and eighteenth centuries. This was that the local gentry should run the local community without undue interference from central government. In a curious way, the major-generals' rule was a re-run of the attempt by Charles I and Laud to interfere with the gentry's control over their communities, and with the localism inherent in English life.

Even for those below the ranks of the gentry the major-generals' rule had positive and negative aspects. It is likely that attempts to make sure the Poor Law was properly administered had a beneficial effect on the rural poor, as did, for example, Whalley's attempt to prevent enclosure of common land. On the other hand, interference with age-old festivals and celebrations such as May Day, and the closing of alehouses, would have been resented. The major-generals were seen as prying Puritan bigots, low-born 'satraps and bashaws', names given to provincial governors in the Ottoman Empire. The memory of their rule, whatever the truth, was one of military dictatorship. It did much to harm Cromwell's attempt to reach an understanding with the political nation of the traditional gentry.

PROBLEMS FOR THE PROTECTORATE

At the same time as the major-generals' experiment other events seemed to demonstrate that Cromwell was becoming more dictatorial. A merchant, George Cony, had refused to pay customs duties on imported silk on the grounds that the duties had not been approved by Parliament. In an action that was reminiscent of Charles I, he and his lawyers were imprisoned for questioning the Protector's authority. Censorship of the press was also tightened up and judges were put under pressure in cases that seemed to challenge the Instrument of Government. However, even if Cromwell was minded to move in a more dictatorial direction (and that is by no means certain), he may have been simply reacting to events. The regime's shortage of money meant that a new parliament would have to be called, but this parliament would be hostile to the major-generals.

Parliament sat infrequently. Therefore it is just as important to look at the situation in the counties, at the local level, as it is to look at the reactions in Parliament to Cromwellian rule. The picture at local level is mixed. Many gentry had refused utterly to take up posts within county government because of the Rump's insistence that all office holders should sign the Engagement. The repeal of the Engagement allowed many gentry, dubious of the legality of republican regimes, to resume their places in county government with a clear conscience. But the major-generals did much to interrupt any rapprochement between the Protectorate and the traditional gentry of the counties – 'I love old England very well' wrote Sir Ralph Verney, 'but as things are carried on here the gentry cannot enjoy much to be in it.' By 1657, however, some of the damage done by the major-generals was beginning to be repaired. Members of families with Royalist sympathies, such as the Berkeleys, had become JPs, joining those from moderate Parliamentarian backgrounds who had disapproved of all the changes from 1648 onwards. On the other hand, many of the gentry were still reluctant to involve themselves in the militia or to consider standing for Parliament. Some were prepared to serve in local government for the sake of their status in the local community, yet could not bring themselves to attend Protectorate Parliaments. The very shortness of the period makes it hard to estimate how many more might have been reconciled to the regime as time went on, or even become positive Cromwellians like Broghill, Onslow and Coplestone. These solid members of the ruling elite saw Cromwell as a force for stability and supported him.

CONCLUSION

The Instrument of Government was a skilful constitutional settlement. It seemed to offer some reforms while bringing back an element of single-person government; indeed, the first idea had been limited kingship. It failed to provide a durable settlement because of opposition not from Royalists but from a mixture of conservative country gentlemen on one side and radicals and Commonwealth's-men on the other. It is possible that time might have reconciled the country gentry to the new constitution, but the existence of the army remained a stumbling block which, by initiating the rule of the major-generals, Cromwell had made a stark issue. Arguably, the system of major-generals was the biggest mistake he made in his quest for 'healing and settling'. On the other hand, outright enemies of the regime, hard-line Royalists as well as Commonwealth's-men, remained in a minority, unable to unseat the Protectorate; and an increasing number of the gentry saw Cromwell as a force for stability and good government. The 'Cromwellians' looked to him as the only possible head of state able to stabilise the country. In general, it can be claimed that, despite all its problems, Cromwell's Protectorate provided stability and at least the semblance of a balance between military and civilian interests. Without Cromwell there was the real possibility of another civil war, an outright military dictatorship, or a slide into anarchy. It was no mean achievement to prevent this.

SECTION 7

Why was Cromwell offered the Crown in 1657, and why did he refuse it?

KEY THEMES

- With the failure of the major-generals' 'experiment' the traditional gentry in the Second Protectorate Parliament and other influential figures concluded that a more conservative settlement was needed.
- For many, kingship was the traditional form of government, but the Restoration of Charles Stuart was impossible.
- In these circumstances only one figure could possibly become king, Cromwell. A Cromwellian monarchy, it was hoped, would provide stability, have more legal force and contain radicals within the army.

THE OFFER OF THE CROWN

The conservatives in the Second Protectorate Parliament were in the majority because more than 100 MPs regarded as Commonwealth's-men had been excluded. These conservative MPs were anxious to return to a traditional mode of government; the known constitutional settlement abandoned only seven years before was monarchy. They could not offer the Crown to the son of Charles I: he was in exile, was an unknown quantity, and rumours suggested he might be a secret Roman Catholic. Indeed, a Stuart restoration might precipitate another civil war because many powerful groups including, of course the army, would be totally opposed to it. And a Stuart restoration might bring Royalist revenge on all those who had fought against Charles I; many people might find themselves in danger of losing their estates, or even worse.

Yet, kingship was the traditional, accepted, legal form of government. Kings had been deposed before and sovereigns crowned who had had fairly vague claims to the throne. In fact the 'right of conquest' was seen, by some, as a legal basis for a claim to the throne. Cromwell could become king and some Royalists would see it as a return to the 'old ways' and accept an Olivarian kingship. Only fanatical Stuart Royalists among the gentry, a small minority, would continue their opposition. Edward Hyde, later Earl of Clarendon, Charles II's closest adviser in exile, actually thought that if Cromwell accepted the Crown Royalism was doomed to a slow decline. Penruddock, who was executed in 1655, said that his revolt would have been treason if Cromwell had been a crowned king.

There were, therefore, strong logical reasons behind Parliament's offer of
the Crown under the leadership of Sir Richard Onslow, a Surrey MP, and
Lord Broghill, the influential former Royalist Anglo-Irish Cromwellian.

When the Second Protectorate Parliament was called in September 1656,
Cromwell was faced with an attack on the major-generals. Oddly, it was a
group of senior officers who had persuaded Cromwell to call Parliament,
not realising the unpopularity of the army.

From the beginning, Parliament, with its cry of 'No Swordsmen, No
Decimators', set out to bring down the major-generals. Their few allies,
such as the pliant and devious member of the Council, Sir Gilbert
Pickering, found themselves exposed. With some regret, Cromwell
abandoned the major-generals' scheme, while still asserting that they had
done good work.

But, by February 1657, he was telling the Council of Officers: 'it is the
time to come to a settlement and lay aside arbitrary proceedings, so
unacceptable to the nation'. It appears that the side of Cromwell that was
'conservative country gentleman' had reasserted itself. He saw himself as
'the good constable of the parish' trying to keep order. He wanted to
build bridges to the traditional political nation, listening to Cromwellians
such as Lord Broghill and the former Royalist Viscount Fauconberg, who
married into the Protector's family. That said, it was also his belief in
religious toleration that made him see the Instrument as having flaws.
The case of James Naylor deeply affected Cromwell. Naylor was a Quaker
preacher who approached Bristol by imitating Christ's entry into
Jerusalem. Parliament savagely punished him for blasphemy by having his
tongue bored, branding and then imprisonment. Cromwell saw Naylor as
merely a deluded man, yet under the Instrument he could offer him no
protection from Parliament's punishment.

WHY DID CROMWELL REFUSE THE CROWN?

At first, Cromwell could see considerable advantages in becoming king.
He had said himself that he was 'not wedded and glued' to forms of
government and, as early as 1652, if Bulstrode Whitelocke, later
ambassador to Sweden, can be relied on, he had mused: 'what if a man
should take it on himself to be king?' He had certainly tried to retain
monarchy up to 1648. Even after the Second Civil War he appeared to
have wavered for a brief time over the trial and execution of Charles I. He
was a republican as a result of his experiences, rather than a republican by
conviction, such as Sir Henry Vane.

However, there were probably three factors that influenced his decision to
refuse the Crown:

- The first was practical. Although the army was loyal to him and he could normally control it, it was republican, seeing itself as the repository and epitome of the republican 'good old cause' for which the Civil Wars had been fought. The army might well revolt at the prospect of King Oliver. Therefore, anarchy rather than stability would be the result of his taking the Crown, and his own position would be precarious.
- On a sentimental level, he shared some of the army's attitudes. A letter from an old soldier, William Bradford, has the essence of this 'sentimental' appeal: 'I beg and beseech your Highness … to consider what you are doing … those that are for a crown, I fear you have little experience of them, the others [opposed to kingship] have attended your greatest hazards … I am of that number … that still loves you … I having gone along with you from Edgehill to Dunbar.' The soldiers and officers of the army were his old comrades with whom he had shared all the dangers of war; if they were against kingship, it must have weighed with him.
- With his belief in the providence of God, the execution of the king in which he had been a prime mover was, to Cromwell, part of God's purpose. Charles I had been a man 'against whom God had witnessed' and God had used Cromwell as his instrument to destroy monarchy. Also, as the man seen as being the destroyer of monarchy, to become king now would be an act of total apostasy. Petitions against monarchy, organised by Colonel Pride, were accumulating in the army around London. Perhaps Cromwell coldly calculated that monarchy was a step too far, even for the army over which he had so much influence.

THE HUMBLE PETITION AND ADVICE

For a mixture of reasons – religious, sentimental and practical – Cromwell refused the Crown in May 1657. However, a modified form of the Parliament's Humble Petition and Advice was accepted by him. It made him, in some ways, king in all but name.

The main points were:

- an 'Upper House' of 40
- the great offices of state and councillors to be approved by Parliament
- biennial Parliaments
- the Protector to name his successor
- members to be excluded from Parliament only by vote of Parliament
- a yearly revenue of £1,300,000: £1 million for the army and navy, £300,000 for support of the government.

Why was Cromwell offered the Crown in 1657, and why did he refuse it?

After the Humble Petition, Cromwell seems to have become a more monarchical and less accessible figure, with a court. The reaction of the army was muted. Major-General Lambert, 'Cromwell's understudy' who had drawn up the original Instrument of Government, refused to accept the Humble Petition and was forced to resign, but with a large pension as a sweetener. Few followed him into the wilderness; only Colonel Packer and five captains resigned. The weak-willed Fleetwood, commander in chief and Cromwell's son-in-law, made noises about resignation, but typically did not give up his command. The army in general did not welcome the change, but some of the senior officers were reassured that its interests would be protected: they would sit in the new Upper House. Cromwell had ridden out the storm, but those who yearned for the 'good old cause', and who were already very uneasy that Cromwell had assumed the Protectorate, saw him as an apostate.

Some, such as Edmund Ludlow – soldier and politician – regarded the whole affair as the climax of a long-planned rise to power:

> the usurper having governed as he thought long enough by virtue of the Instrument of Government, which though drawn up by himself and his creatures, was now thought to lay too great a restraint upon his ambitious spirit, and resolving to rest satisfied with nothing less than the succession of his family to the crown, he attempted to make himself king.

In some ways the Humble Petition and Advice satisfied no one group in the widely divided political spectrum. The conservatives thought that nothing but a return to the old 'known way' of monarchy would provide a durable settlement; the republicans saw enough of kingship in the Petition to dislike it intensely. Cromwell hoped that this compromise would provide a settlement: 'You have need to look at settlement … for the nation needs it and never needed it more … I am hugely taken with the word settlement, with the thing and with the notion of it.'

The second session of Parliament in January 1658 showed how elusive that settlement was proving. The new Upper House of Forty was partly composed of 'Cromwellians' from the Lower House, such as Broghill, Whitelocke and Onslow. Some of Cromwell's old allies such as Lord Saye and Sele and Oliver St John refused places in the Upper House on principle. With the departure of the likes of Broghill and Onslow, the Lower House lacked a strong, influential 'Cromwellian' group. At the same time, the Humble Petition had removed the right to block MPs from sitting, so the Commonwealth's-men returned, determined to attack the constitution and to restore the Rump, however vain a hope that might be.

Attacks on the new Upper House came from all sides. For the Commonwealth's-men, it was a return to what had been abolished in 1649; a return to, in Heselrige's words, 'bondage in Egypt'. Some landed MPs saw some of the Upper House, especially the army officers, as men with no stake in the country, not financially independent, 'mean people who must be paid by you'. Cromwell lost patience and within a month dissolved Parliament, after a speech defending the Upper House: 'I named it out of men that can meet you wheresoever you go, and shake hands with you and tell you it is not titles … they value but a Christian and English interest.' He ended by saying: 'Let God judge between you and me.' The Commonwealth's-men replied: 'Amen.'

CROMWELL'S LAST MONTHS

After the dissolution of his last Parliament, Cromwell seems to have become increasingly ill. He probably suffered recurrent attacks of malaria contracted in Ireland. George Fox, the Quaker leader, met him at Hampton Court and spoke of 'a waft of death' about him. The summer of 1658 was full of personal loss: his old friend Warwick and his son-in-law Richard Rich died. Even more shattering was the death of his favourite daughter Elizabeth, Bettie, after an agonising illness, most probably cancer of the stomach.

His political troubles were made more difficult by financial ones. His income as Lord Protector was £1,300,000, which fell short of that needed to pay government expenditure. The shortfall was in the order of £500,000, and the City was not forthcoming with loans. Although ailing, he was still capable of action. He appears to have been planning another purge of the army to remove politically unreliable officers. That this was not complete before his death is of great significance: his son Richard was unable to control the army and this led to his fall and the eventual restoration of Charles II.

Bettie Cromwell. The death of his favourite daughter was a shattering blow to Cromwell.

By 2 September 1658, Cromwell was extremely ill. After naming Richard as his successor, he lapsed in and out of consciousness, praying when awake: 'my work is done but God will be with his people' and 'Thou hast made me, though very unworthy, a mean instrument to do them some good … and many have set too high a value upon me though others … would be glad of my death, Lord however thou do dispose of me, continue and do good for them …'. When offered something to drink he murmured: 'It is not my design to drink or to sleep, but my design is to make what haste I can to be gone.' On the afternoon of 3 September, in a 'great thunderstorm' and on the anniversary of his victories at Dunbar and Worcester, he died.

Why was Cromwell offered the Crown in 1657, and why did he refuse it?   57

CONCLUSION

It can be argued that Cromwell, although disappointed of the high hopes he had in 1653, had ruled efficiently, justly and had provided stability in a very disturbed time. Without a Cromwellian protectorship it is probable that England would have slipped into anarchy and bloodshed. No one else could have performed the task he did.

SECTION 8

Cromwell: key themes

INTRODUCTION

There is no doubting that Cromwell is a controversial figure in history. There are a number of questions about Cromwell that need to be answered:

- Was Cromwell's rule a dictatorship?
- To what extent can Cromwell's career be explained by personal ambition?
- What was Cromwell's record on religious toleration?
- What was Cromwell's record in Ireland?

WAS CROMWELL'S RULE A DICTATORSHIP?

The existence of the large standing army, loyal to the Protector, the major-generals' experiment of 1655–6 and Cromwell's failure to establish good relations with his Parliaments all indicate an element of

Oliver
Cromwell by
Robert Walker.

dictatorship. These have been seen as marking Cromwell's regime out from all other English governments. This view is put in its classic form by **Lucy Hutchinson**: 'Cromwell and his army grew wanton with their power, and invented a thousand tricks of government … several sorts of mock parliaments … he at last exercised such an arbitrary power that the whole land grew weary of him.'

It is certainly true that the army exerted more influence on political life in the 1650s than at any other period in English history, and this created a lasting mistrust of standing armies. It is hard to see how the Protectorate could have survived without the army. **Christopher Hill** puts it bluntly when he writes that, in the last resort, Cromwell's power 'rested on bayonets'. However, it can be argued that, had the army not existed, chaos and/or another civil conflict would have ensued given the divided nature of England in the 1650s. Of course, the existence of this expensive army, which necessitated high taxation and threatened the traditional rights of the gentry to rule their localities, was one of the reasons why a settlement was so difficult to obtain in that period. And the major-generals were seen by many of the gentry as a symbol of military dictatorship.

The truth is, however, more complex. A military dictatorship implies that the army rules without regard for the law; doing what its leader sees fit; riding roughshod over civil rights; imprisoning or executing those who oppose it. Even during the major-generals' experiment this could never be said to be so. Some officers became justices of the peace to give their actions legality, and some saw themselves as representing the interests of the districts, bringing their problems to the notice of central government. They also tried, with varying degrees of success, to work with the existing local gentry government. Haynes in Suffolk, for example, seems to have got on well with the leading gentry; Worsley in Lancashire very badly.

It can be argued that Cromwell's control of the army prevented outright military dictatorship. There were ambitious senior officers, as the events of 1659 showed, who wanted the army to have the controlling interest in the country. It is true to say that the army under Cromwell's leadership, or with his tacit consent, had been responsible for Pride's Purge in 1648 and the dismissal of the Rump in 1653; so it is easy to see the army as having a decisive influence. Certainly, those excluded by Colonel Pride, and the ejected Rumpers thought so and had an abiding dislike and mistrust of the army.

After the dismissal of the Rump and the voluntary dissolution of the Nominated Parliament, there were opportunities for Cromwell to rule as a military dictator. He did not take them. Indeed, even the army could not contemplate a military government after the Rump's dismissal, and set up the Nominated Parliament. The perfectly legal surrender of this Parliament's powers was followed by the Instrument of Government, a constitution that limited the powers of both the army and the Lord Protector. The composition of the Protector's Council laid down in the Instrument gave a majority to civilians; only five of the fifteen named can be seen as officer politicians who would support army influence. They were Lambert, Fleetwood, Desborough, Sydenham and Skippon.

Cromwell, despite his military career, remained in many ways a country gentleman, and therefore always tried to rule according to the 'known laws'. As he pointed out himself, with the resignation of the Nominated Parliament he had 'unlimited' power, yet he accepted the Instrument of Government, which bound him legally. He seems always to have sought to curb army influence, especially after 1653, in order to return to the 'old ways' to settle the country. The senior law officers were, of course, not soldiers, and at local government level only about one in 30 JPs was an army officer.

Cromwell also continued to reduce the size of the army after 1653, from approximately 53,000 to 36,000. Of that 36,000, probably only 14,000 were serving in England itself. This was a large enough number to secure the regime against feeble Royalist plots and uprisings. It could be argued, however, that it was hardly an instrument to oppress a population of five million. Nonetheless, it is true to say that the army had a greater influence than at any other period in English history, but that does not constitute a dictatorship. It must be said, however, that this was the first time in English history when there was a standing army garrisoned all over the country.

Another aspect of dictatorship is a disregard for 'civil rights' and the rule of law. **Marchamont Nedham**, admittedly an ex-Royalist journalist of pliable political principles, described the Instrument of Government as a blend of monarchy, aristocracy and democracy, with Protector, Council and Parliament; in other words, a balanced constitution that was traditional in spirit. Nedham, of course, was an apologist but he had a point. Cromwell's acceptance of the Instrument meant that he had less power than monarchs before 1640, and the Instrument seemed to represent what the Parliamentarians of 1642 had aimed at.

As far as the law was concerned, Cromwell's rule was characterised by continuity with the past. *Cony's* case, involving a merchant who refused to pay taxes not voted by Parliament, is often quoted as an example of Cromwell ignoring the law, like Charles I, but it is famous because it was an exceptional case. Trials by jury were the rule; trials by high courts of justice with nominated commissioners happened more rarely under the Protectorate than during the Rump. The two that occurred between

1654 and 1658 concerned conspiracies: one to assassinate Cromwell, the other a Royalist rising. Even the trials after Penruddock's Rising were jury trials. On a personal level, Cromwell disliked capital punishment, wishing it reserved only for murder. It might be pointed out that the aftermath of Penruddock's Rising saw 39 rebels either executed or transported to Barbados; Around 250 were executed after Monmouth's Rebellion in 1685 during the reign of James II. Elizabeth also had dealt far more harshly with rebels than Cromwell.

Unlike a dictator, Cromwell seems to have been remarkably tolerant of dissent, provided it did not spill over into armed uprising. He held long discussions with those who disagreed with him, even with the much-feared Quaker leader George Fox. It has been said that his belief in religious toleration extended to a tacit toleration of Catholic worship in secret, to the Jews, to allowing Anglican services if they had no 'Royalist' flavour. His parliaments were not as tolerant as he. As far as local government was concerned, military influence during the period, leaving aside the time of the major-generals' rule, was very limited. Probably fewer than 90 officers served as JPs out of a total of perhaps 2500 magistrates. The major-generals' interlude should not be seen as typical of army influence in local affairs during this period.

As far as the 'personal' element of dictatorship is concerned, Cromwell seemed very anxious that decisions should be taken by the Council rather than by him. The Council had far more influence over decisions than credited by those who see Cromwell as an all-powerful figure. The Humble Petition and Advice again shows the dominance of civilians. The army disliked it and the Upper House contained only twelve officers.

Therefore, it cannot be argued that Cromwell was in any fundamental way a dictator. He could, on occasion, act arbitrarily, as with the dismissal of the Rump, whose legal authority could in any case be questioned. But his instinct was to follow the rule of law. His problem was that the existence of the army, and his desire to 'enforce' religious toleration, often put him at odds with the traditional political nation that he tried to woo after 1653. Arguably, Charles I's personal rule, and certainly James II's rule from 1685 to 1688 contain more elements of dictatorship than Cromwell's.

TO WHAT EXTENT CAN CROMWELL'S CAREER BE EXPLAINED BY PERSONAL AMBITION?

The rise from country squire to king in all but name, a career unprecedented in English history, did not result from a series of accidents. Elements of shrewd political calculation were involved. Cromwell also had a strong belief in 'God's providences'. However, the idea that Cromwell planned all his moves, that he schemed and plotted to become Lord Protector and, in 1657, an uncrowned monarch, albeit with limited powers, is an untenable thesis. Such a thesis was held by fanatical Royalist opponents, believers in conspiracy theories, or republicans so disillusioned with Cromwell (people such as Ludlow and Lucy Hutchinson, wife of the regicide Colonel Hutchinson) that their views became distorted.

Cromwell himself once remarked: 'no one goes so far as he who knows not where he goes', and perhaps this offers an explanation of his career. He did not have a deeply laid plot to seize power, but he accepted or took advantage of situations as they arose. Two other points have to be made. First, ambition is not necessarily an ignoble or dishonest motive: many politicians who have done great service to their country or the world have been ambitious, otherwise they would have remained obscure. Second, although Cromwell gained financially out of his military and political career, he was already rich enough to lend Parliament £1000 in 1642, and for most of his life lived fairly simply. Some observers remarked upon the plainness of his dress, and it is not until after the Humble Petition and Advice that he can be seen as having a 'court' living in any 'state' at all.

To answer this question we need to look at turning points in his career, the possible motivations for his actions and the way he took decisions.

The first turning point might be seen to be the Self-denying Ordinance, finally passed in April 1645. There is no doubt that he had prepared the ground with his allies in the houses of Commons and Lords but he took a risk that he and other MP officers would find themselves out of the army. Manchester accused him of insubordination and of building up a 'party' of Independents within the army. These were very damaging charges to be aired in public and Parliament might well have decided that both Manchester and Cromwell were a liability and brought them both down. Incidentally, Manchester's charges were not completely convincing; it is true that Cromwell promoted Independents, but he also promoted Presbyterians if they were not of the hard-line, intolerant variety. Cromwell later seems to have taken Waller's orders without question, because he regarded him as being, unlike Manchester, a competent commander. He may have calculated that Parliament would give him exemption from the Ordinance, given his successful military career. But he could not be sure of that; therefore, it is possible that he acted in what he saw as the public interest, and took the risk that he would lose his command, but at least generals who were competent and wanted to win it would direct the war.

The seizure of the king was another crucial moment in Cromwell's career. Cornet Joyce with 500 horsemen took Charles from Holdenby House where he was under Parliamentary house arrest and brought him to the army. Cromwell claimed to know nothing of the action until afterwards, but it seems unlikely that a mere cornet, the lowest officer rank in the army, would act without at least the tacit support of his superior officers. Given that Charles was negotiating with the army's (and Cromwell's) political opponents, the Presbyterians in Parliament, it was vital to boost the army's interests by negotiating with Charles directly, in order to prevent a Presbyterian anti-army settlement. So, at the very least, the seizure of the king was in Cromwell's interest; not in terms of personal ambition but in terms of the settlement that he and the army wanted. At the time some thought that Charles' escape from the army and flight to Carisbrooke had been with the connivance of Cromwell. There is little if any hard evidence to support the idea that Cromwell let Charles escape in order to trap him, as the poet Marvell wrote in his contemporary poem 'an Horatian Ode upon Cromwell's return from Ireland'.

The putting down of the Leveller mutineers can be seen as the destruction of a threat to Cromwell's position within the army. Yet, arguably, Cromwell's main consideration now that he had thrown in his lot with the army against Parliamentary Presbyterians, was to keep the army together. A collapse into internal divisions would not only lead to chaos at a time of acute crisis, but would also favour only the Parliamentarians who wanted to disband the army, or the Royalists. Of course, a divided army would not be in Cromwell's interest, but his main objection to the ideas of the Levellers, at this time, seems to have been that their idea of democracy would lead to anarchy.

Pride's Purge appears to have been instigated by Ireton and the other senior officers. Cromwell was still in Yorkshire, but he expressed his approval of the Purge once he arrived in London. Perhaps he hoped to avoid the odium of being associated with an illegal purge of Parliament, while seeing the necessity and advantage of it. As for the trial and execution of Charles, it was not the result of Cromwell's scheming for Charles' head but of the realisation by some that the Second Civil War had shown that Charles was devious and prepared to do anything to recover his powers. Indeed, if Cromwell had wished to save the king's life, it is doubtful that he could have swayed the Council of Officers and the army. They were determined to bring 'Charles Stuart that man of blood to an account for the blood he had shed'. There is, anyway, little evidence that Cromwell ever seriously thought of saving the king.

The dismissal of the Rump in 1653 is perhaps the most controversial act of Cromwell's career. He was already the arbiter of affairs, the leading member of the Council of State and commander of the army, and the dismissal of the Rump gave him the potential for absolute power. His motives for dismissing the Rump have already been discussed. It should also be noted that Lambert, who led the army officer 'politiques' and was thinking of a new settled constitution, and Major-General Harrison, who saw the Rump as a godless assembly preventing the establishment of the new Jerusalem in England, both wanted to get rid of the Rump. The army, though divided, pushed Cromwell into; he did not push the army.

Once the Rump was dismissed, Cromwell rejected a military dictatorship. He later remarked: 'I say, the authority I had in my hands being so boundless as it was, I being by act of Parliament General of all the forces in the three nations of England, Scotland and Ireland – in which unlimited condition I did not desire to live a day.' He, with the Council of Officers, nominated an assembly, the Nominated Parliament, which had wide powers and was by no means a tool of either Cromwell or the army.

As far as his assumption of the protectorship in December 1653 is concerned, several points can be made. The actual resignation of the Nominated Parliament and handover of its power back to him was, he asserted, a surprise: 'I knew not one tittle of it.' This is not convincing. At the very least, Lambert and his civilian allies in Parliament must have had some idea that Cromwell would accept the protectorship and that he would accept a new constitution. On the other hand, his ambition did not stretch to the kingship that was originally offered. He claimed that he was persuaded to become Protector: 'they told me that except I would undertake the government, they thought things could hardly come to a composure, a settlement, but blood and confusion could break in upon us'. He also pointed out that, again he had rejected absolute power:

> *I confess after many arguments and after letting of me know that I did not receive anything that put me into a higher capacity than I was in before, but that it limited me and bound my hands to act nothing to the prejudice of the nations without the consent of a council until Parliament met, and then limited me by the Parliament … I did accept it.*

It might be said that Cromwell's rise to power had made him the only possible choice as head of State, and shrewd political sense had assisted that rise. But he was certainly sincere in his assertion that he could have had absolute power and had rejected it. He may have seen that he was the only possible choice and that only a Cromwellian protectorate stood between a divided nation and anarchy, so it was his 'God-given' duty to 'undertake the government'.

Cromwell's acceptance of the Humble Petition and Advice can be seen as proof of his ambitions. Although he rejected kingship, the amended petition still gave him the right to name his successor, who would certainly be a Cromwell. His investiture bore all the marks of previous royal coronations, including sword, sceptre and purple robe. However, given his own desire for 'healing and settling', and his wish to build bridges to the traditional gentry, then if he could not accept kingship, a protectorate with the trappings was the least, politically, that could be done. Of course, for many of Cromwell's old friends and comrades in the army and former Parliamentarian allies it was the ultimate apostasy: a symbol of how Cromwell had betrayed 'the good old cause' for his own personal ambition.

It is difficult to come to a definite conclusion on the question of Cromwell's ambition. On many occasions he seems not to have been a determined schemer but to have been torn between differing courses of action by moral uncertainty. He spent hours in contemplation and prayer 'waiting on the Lord', and then made up his mind and acted decisively. Like many seventeenth-century Puritans, Cromwell believed that God's will would show itself; that divine favour would come to those who followed God's will, which would be revealed through prayer and events. God would choose men to do his will and Cromwell believed he was one of the chosen: 'I am one of those whose heart God hath drawn out to wait for some extraordinary dispensations.' Once he was convinced that he was doing the Lord's work, he acted, seeing himself as an agent of God's will. Of course, God often seemed to indicate a course of action to Cromwell that was in his interest.

To his opponents, Cromwell's references to 'God's providences' were smokescreens of piety to cover up devious political changes of principle for personal advantage. Given the deeply held religious beliefs of the time, it is fruitless to pin a charge of hypocrisy on Cromwell any more than on his equally religious opponents.

The question of Cromwell's ambition is one that has exercised contemporaries and historians alike, and there can be no certain answer. If he was ambitious and he used events to further this ambition, he certainly retained some of his principles, such as opposition to absolutist government and belief in religious toleration, and remained remarkably modest and open-minded, even with his opponents.

Whether he was a 'brave bad man', carving out a career in bloody and troubled times, or the 'great captain' incorruptible in essentials, only reluctantly taking power for the good of 'God's people', must be decided by the reader, preferably after more reading and study.

WHAT WAS CROMWELL'S RECORD ON RELIGIOUS TOLERATION?

Religion was a central part of Cromwell's life and thought from his conversion in the early 1630s. In some ways he was a conventional

Calvinist Puritan, believing in predestination and spending much time in prayer. However, unlike most of his contemporaries, he did not think that his beliefs were the only valid ones.

From before the beginning of the Civil War he took a broadly tolerant attitude. As early as February 1641 he was enquiring about 'the reasons of the Scots to enforce their discipline of uniformity in religion'. In 1644 he clashed with a strict Scottish Presbyterian, Major-General Crawford in the Eastern Association, who had dismissed an officer for being an Anabaptist. Cromwell wrote to him: 'Admit he be, shall that render him incapable to serve the public? Sir, the state in choosing men to serve them takes no notice of their opinions, if they be willing … to serve, that satisfies.'

In September 1645 he wrote to the Speaker after the taking of Bristol that 'Presbyterians, Independents all had here the same spirit of faith and prayer … they agree here to know no names of difference, pity it is it should be otherwise anywhere.' At the same time he had come to see that strict Scottish Presbyterianism was as intolerant as the Laudian Anglican Church.

In 1646, he found time to write to a former Royalist in Norfolk, Sir Thomas Knyvett, who had a rich tenant who had threatened to evict some poor sub-tenants because of their unconventional religious beliefs:

> The trouble I hear [is that] *they are like to suffer for their consciences. And however the world interprets it, I am not ashamed to solicit for such as are anywhere under a pressure of this kind, doing herein as I would be done by. Sir, this is a quarrelsome age, and the anger seems to me to be the worse, where the ground is things of difference in opinion which to cure, to hurt men in their names, persons or estates will not be found an apt remedy.*

For Cromwell, religious toleration meant not only that men might find their way to God in various beliefs, but it also made political sense: it prevented disorder and promoted harmony. It fits in with Cromwell's other preoccupations: fear of anarchy and desire for settlement.

To the general assembly of the Scottish Presbyterian Kirk in 1650 he wrote memorably: 'it is therefore infallibly agreeable to the Word of God, all that you say? I beseech you, in the bowels of Christ think it possible you may be mistaken.' And to the governor of Edinburgh castle: 'Your pretended fear lest error should step in, is like the man who would keep all the wine out of the country lest men should be drunk.'

Cromwell was not the only Puritan to support the readmittance of the Jews in 1655. The famous minister and regicide Hugh Peter had suggested 'Jews being admitted to trade and live amongst us'. In 1651, Thurloe had met Menasseh Ben Israel, leader of the Amsterdam Jewish community, and suggested that he apply to the Council for Jews to resettle in England. Cromwell's invitation to the Jews was based on two strands of thinking: religious toleration and trade. He saw the Jews as being one of the reasons for Amsterdam's financial success. It is perhaps typical of the intolerance that Cromwell struggled against that many regarded the unofficial return of the Jews with distaste or worse. Prynne, the Presbyterian pamphleteer and excluded member, was violently anti-Semitic, as well as intolerant to all who did not share his narrow Presbyterianism. He accused Cromwell of having been bribed by the Jews with a gift of £20,000, a quite ludicrous assertion.

As far as the Quakers were concerned, Cromwell's attitude, unlike most, was one of cautious toleration within limits. As early as 1654, George Fox was released by him after Fox had promised not to 'take up a carnal sword' against the government. He continued to meet Fox in the following years and to try to release imprisoned Quakers, provided they had not been involved in disturbances against the peace. Some Quakers were, of course, violent; and some of Cromwell's associates certainly did not share his tolerant attitudes. Major-General Boteler took every opportunity to imprison Quakers during his control of Northamptonshire, and the Cromwellian General Monck had no time for them, purging them from the army in Scotland.

As far as the Anglicans were concerned, Cromwell seems to have tried to allow them a degree of tacit toleration, provided their services were not fronts for Royalist conspiracy. He was personally close to Archbishop Usher of Armagh, whose funeral was paid for out of state funds, with an Anglican service in Westminster Abbey. It has already been noted that, in practical terms, Catholics, like Anglicans, enjoyed a degree of tacit toleration, albeit to a lesser extent: the French ambassador remarked that Catholics enjoyed more practical toleration than they had under Charles I.

However, the Naylor case showed that the majority of Parliament did not share the Protector's tolerance, and Cromwell could not force people to be tolerant. Religious toleration was a rare quality in the seventeenth century and, in some respects, it puts Cromwell ahead of his time. It is also the only principle from which he seems never to have wavered throughout his career. The survival of English nonconformity and the reputation of the English for tolerance is part of his abiding legacy.

WHAT WAS CROMWELL'S RECORD IN IRELAND?

The traditional view of Cromwell's campaign in Ireland is that of a bloodthirsty conquest, accompanied by massacres of the population, that has left an enduring folk memory of the 'curse of Cromwell'.

There are reasons for this view that have little to do with historical fact and a lot to do with the religious and political divisions of Ireland, and the English attitude to Ireland. It can be argued that, from the beginning of the English ascendancy over Ireland, English policy towards the native Celtic Catholic Irish was not, in any way, enlightened. Cromwell has been used as a scapegoat for all the Anglo-Irish problems. Legends rather than objective history have resulted and these distorted views have governed the view of Cromwell's campaigns in Ireland. Recent research by **Ronald Hutton**, and in greater detail by an Irish local historian **Tom Reilly**, set out in his book *Cromwell an Honourable Enemy* (1999), has modified the traditional picture.

There was a history of inhumane conduct in Ireland long before Cromwell arrived in 1649. Sir Francis Drake, for example, seen as the archetypical Elizabethan hero, massacred Irish women and children at Rathlin Island in 1575. The killing of Protestant settlers by the Catholic rebels in 1641 was certainly the largest single incident of its type in the history of England, Scotland or Ireland; between 3000 and 5000 people died. But these figures were wildly exaggerated in London in late 1641. It is also important to understand whom Cromwell was actually fighting in 1649. It is a complicated picture. The 'confederates' against the new republic were composed of native Celtic Irish Catholic rebels from 1641 and Royalist Anglo-Irish Protestants and Catholics. There were considerable tensions and suspicions between the two groups within this Catholic–Royalist coalition. For example, one of the most influential Celtic chiefs Muireadhach O'Brien, Lord Inchquin, had fought for Parliament until 1648, and some of the Royalist commander Ormonde's troops were not in any sense Irish at all, but Royalist refugees. So two strands were coming together, often not co-operating fully: first, straightforward Royalism, of the sort that had already been defeated in the two Civil Wars in England; and, second, Irish Catholic 'nationalist' rebels. Often the latter would not allow Royalists to defend their towns and these divisions certainly helped Cromwell and his successors in Ireland to subjugate the country.

By the time Cromwell had landed with 10,000 men in Ireland in August 1649, the confederate leader Ormonde had already been defeated by Michael Jones, the governor of Dublin, at Rathmines, so his task was easier. Before Cromwell left for Ireland he had made it clear that he saw it as the greatest threat: 'they will in a very short time be able to land forces in England ... I had rather be over-run with a Cavalierish interest than a Scotch interest, I had rather been over-run with a Scotch interest than an Irish interest, and I think of all this is the most dangerous.'

The sieges of Drogheda in September and Wexford in October have been portrayed as showing that he put this fear and hostility into action by massacres on a scale unknown before, massacres that involved large numbers of civilians. The fate of the two towns has gone down as being the greatest stain on Cromwell's reputation; some accounts even suggest that the entire population of the towns was killed. However, at Drogheda only those 'under arms' – combatants – were killed: normal seventeenth-century practice if a besieged garrison refused to surrender and the attackers then forced their way into the town. In any case, surrender was virtually impossible once the besiegers entered a town and hand to hand fighting took place. The garrison at Drogheda was not mainly composed of Irish Catholics; they were English Royalists, and their continued resistance was seen as prolonging the Civil War. The refusal to surrender inevitably led to 'no quarter' when Cromwell's troops finally stormed the town. In *A Concise History of Ireland* (1972), **Maire O'Brien** points out: 'from a military point of view, the ferocity of Cromwell and his successors in Ireland, Ireton and Ludlow, was not extraordinary by seventeenth-century military standards. The action of Cromwell's which lingers in the folk memory – the sack of Drogheda – was hardly more ferocious or macabre than that of Cashel by ... the Earl of Inchquin in 1646.' There is no evidence that women and children died at Drogheda. The death of Sir Arthur Aston, the commander at Drogheda, was no more horrible and terrible than the deaths of the Parliamentary defenders of Leicester at the hands of Prince Rupert in 1645, or the Royalist defenders of Colchester in 1648, such as Sir Charles Lucas, shot on the orders of the normally chivalrous Sir Thomas Fairfax.

As far as Wexford is concerned, the same slaughter of defenders occurred, but the deaths of women and children that Cromwell was blamed for were not at the hand of his troops: they drowned in overloaded boats while trying to escape.

The commander at Wexford, Colonel David Sinnott, had actually spun out the negotiations for the town's surrender while hoping for reinforcements, and Cromwell showed remarkable patience in continuing to parley with him rather than ordering an immediate assault. His last letter to Sinnott ran as follows:

> *Sir, I have had the patience to peruse yon propositions, to which I might have returned an answer with some distain. But, to be short, I shall give the soldiers and non-commissioned officers quarter for life and leave to go to their several habitations ... they engaging to take up arms no more with*

*the Parliament of England, and the commissioned officers for their lives to
render themselves prisoners. As for the inhabitants, I shall engage myself
that no violence shall be offered to their goods and that I shall protect their
town from plunder.*

Sinnott probably never received this final communication because the
commander of the castle seems suddenly to have allowed the
Parliamentarian troops to take it, and almost immediately they stormed
the rest of the town. Cromwell was in his tent at this point and had no
control over his troops. Where Cromwell can indeed be blamed is that in
the one hour of slaughter that followed he made no effort to prevent
about 1500 defenders including some Catholic priests from being killed.

Cromwell's justification for the slaughter of these two garrisons was
exactly the same as the justification for dropping the atom bombs on
Hiroshima and Nagasaki at the end of the Second World War. By such
acts of terror the war would be ended earlier and, as he wrote to the
Speaker of the House of Commons, 'further effusion of blood' would be
prevented. This is not to excuse Cromwell, but to put the Drogheda and
Wexford sieges in context in terms of seventeenth-century military
practice and in terms of morality – however dubious. Cromwell was no
better or worse than other military commanders of his age. Indeed, given
the horrors of the twentieth century with the indiscriminate bombing of
civilians from the air practised by all sides in war, Cromwell and his
fellow seventeenth-century military commanders seem positively merciful.
It suited both Irish nationalist historians of the nineteenth century and
post-Restoration English historians who used every opportunity to
blacken Cromwell's name, and perhaps blame Ireland's problems on him,
to portray him as uniquely culpable. But the hard evidence is against
them.

The sieges of Drogheda and Wexford did not entirely break the back of
the confederates' resistance. Indeed, Cromwell suffered a severe setback at
Clonmel, arguably the worst in his military career, with 2000 casualties
before he could leave 'mopping up' operations to Ireton and Ludlow.
Ireland became part of the Commonwealth. Confiscations of land finally
broke the Catholics as a land-owning force: In 1641, Catholics owned 59
per cent of the land, by 1653 they had only 20 per cent. This ruthless
supplanting of native Catholic landowners by Protestants was not
Cromwell's policy as much as the policy of the Rump designed to ensure
that Celtic Catholicism could never again be a threat to English
domination of Ireland. It left a very bitter legacy, and was in real terms
far more damaging to Anglo-Irish relations than myths about the unique
nature of Cromwell's ruthlessness towards the Irish in battle.

Given that Cromwell's conduct in Ireland has been such an emotive topic, the reader is urged to consult further, the most 'revisionist' texts being **Toby Barnard**'s article 'Irish Images of Cromwell' in *Images of Oliver Cromwell*, ed. R.C. Richardson (Manchester, 1993) and the already mentioned *Cromwell an Honourable Enemy*, by **Tom Reilly**.

On the question of surrender of garrisons, **Richard Holmes** in *Redcoat* (1999) remarks that even later in the eighteenth and early nineteenth centuries 'the rules of war were clear enough. Once a breach (in the walls) was practicable and indefensible, and … assault imminent the Governor had to surrender or accept that he and his men would receive no quarter and that the town in his charge would be given over to pillage … the custom was designed to prevent useless slaughter.'

Therefore it can be argued that Cromwell's record in Ireland is not a uniquely black one and that the 'myth' of Cromwell and the 'curse' of his campaign is just that. Myths, however, are often more significant in shaping attitudes than the truth.

PART 2: ANALYSIS AND INTERPRETATION

SECTION 9

Historical sources and historiography

SOURCES

There are various kinds of sources for the period. If possible, it can be most useful to know the bias and the political and/or religious stance of the writer.

Diaries
These are sometimes private journals that record the thoughts of people and the way they saw events. You might come across the diary of Ralph Josselin 1645–60; Josselin was a Puritan vicar of Earls Colne in Essex who supported Parliament but was horrified at the death of the king. The Quaker George Fox also kept a journal. Some diaries and journals are better informed about national events, for example private journals of the Long Parliament: see the diary of Thomas Burton and the journal of Sir Simonds D'Ewes. There is also an 'official' Commons journal.

The thoughts of individuals written down by others include the famous John Selden's *Table Talk*. Selden was a distinguished lawyer who opposed the king but at the same time saw the faults of the king's opponents. He was one of the most detached observers of the time.

Official documents
There are official documents regarding the constitution, laws and instructions to major-generals and justices of the peace. The Clarke Papers contain not only Clarke's own writings as secretary to the Council of the Army 1640–9, and secretary to General Monck 1651–60, but also reports and letters.

Documents of government officers
The Calendar of State Papers Venetian (CSPV) is a valuable source. The Venetian ambassadors reported once a week at great length to the Doge of Venice; they were shrewd, well-informed observers who can to a large degree be seen as neutral. John Thurloe, secretary of state 1652–60, was a loyal Cromwellian who left several volumes of important papers, reports and letters. Thurloe made it his business to be very well informed and ran an extensive intelligence network, breaking plots against Cromwell's life. His own sympathies are clear from his letters.

Contemporary accounts

Several contemporaries wrote their account of the events of the period, coloured of course by their own prejudices. The longest, fullest and most accurate is Clarendon's *History of the Great Rebellion*. Clarendon was a constitutional Royalist who opposed Charles' policies in the 1630s, but had joined the Royalist cause by late 1641. His pen portraits of individuals can be sardonic and perhaps biased, but his grasp of the facts is usually very sound. However, in the 1650s he was an exile abroad with Charles II, and not, therefore, a first-hand observer of events. Edmund Ludlow, a republican Wiltshire gentleman, wrote his memoirs after 1660 while in exile. He had been a leading figure in public life until 1654 when he broke with Cromwell over Cromwell's assumption of the protectorship, which he regarded as a betrayal of the republican cause. Lucy Hutchinson, who wrote *The Life of Colonel Hutchinson*, was another republican Puritan who came to see Cromwell as an ambitious schemer who had betrayed 'the good old cause'. She disliked the lower-class army officers and was also anxious to justify the career of her husband, a regicide republican. Bulstrode Whitelocke wrote his *Memorials of English Affairs* after the Restoration. Whitelocke was a distinguished lawyer, sitting in both Protectorate Parliaments after a spell as ambassador to Sweden. He was chair of the committee appointed to urge Cromwell to accept the Crown, and afterwards served both Richard Cromwell and the army-controlled Committee of Safety in 1659. With the restoration of Charles II he was, of course, anxious to distance himself from Cromwell and he seems to have been a rather devious figure. He was, however, in the centre of events in the late 1640s, the Commonwealth and the Protectorate. The autobiography of Richard Baxter is another valuable source for the period. Baxter was a Puritan minister, an army chaplain in 1644–5, and in the 1650s worked for unity between Anglicans, Presbyterians and Independents. He was a shrewd observer, opining that Cromwell wished to do good but was also ambitious.

There are short accounts of Cromwell written after the Restoration. Not surprisingly, they are hostile. One of the best-known, Slingsby Bethel's *The World's Mistake in Oliver Cromwell*, was published in 1668. Bethel, an ex-Rumper, was anxious to defend the Rump's record and attack Cromwell who had of course dismissed the Rump. His attack is mainly on Cromwell's foreign policy but also on his character and his 'pretended Protectorship'.

Newsbooks

With the virtual ending of censorship in 1640, there was an explosion of what nowadays could be called newspapers – newsbooks. Some ran only for one or two issues, others over a long period of time. By 1645 there were 722 newsbooks. Some read very much like the modern tabloid press: full of murders and sexual scandals. Others were highly political in nature, attempting to present propaganda as news. During the Civil War the three main Royalist newsbooks were *Mercurius Aulicus*, *Mercurius Rusticas* and *Mercurius Pragmaticus*. The last named was the product of Marchamont Nedham, an opportunist journalist, who later changed sides and wrote for the Commonwealth and Protectorate. *Mercurius Politicus* and the *Moderate Intelligencer* were Parliamentary productions, as was *Mercurius Britannicus*. *Mercurius Politicus* can be read as almost the official voice of the regimes of the 1650s.

Pamphlets

The Levellers produced their own pamphlets; first calling for reform and then after 1650 expressing disappointment with the failure of the Rump to produce any, later attacking Cromwell for betraying the revolution. The most extreme was Sexby's famous defence of tyrannicide (the assassination of a tyrant, in this case Cromwell) in *Killing no Murder*. The main Leveller writers were John Lilburne, William Walwyn and Richard Overton. Gerard Winstanley, the Digger leader, also addressed pleas to Cromwell, hoping to persuade him to use his power in 1650–1 to create a radical reform of society.

Speeches

There are of course Cromwell's own speeches. They tend to be hesitant and repetitive. Often they seem to be concerned not only with Cromwell's hopes and beliefs but also attempts to justify himself, particularly regarding accusations of hypocrisy and ambition. They should be read with caution and not uncritically.

Assessing sources

If you have some idea of the prejudices and attitudes of the writer, it can be most helpful when assessing seventeenth-century documents (as with any other period). The language used can also give clues to the views of the writer. References to Cromwell that call him 'His Highness' or 'the Lord General', 'Our Chief of Men' (unless used ironically) indicate approval. Phrases such as 'the Usurper', 'Tyrant', and 'Apostate' of course indicate the opposite. The words 'mean', 'low-born', 'satraps' and 'bashaws' were used by conservative Royalist or Presbyterian gentry to show their contempt for the social inferiority of Cromwell's officers and are indications of hostility. On the other hand, the term 'grandee' was used by the Levellers to describe senior officers in the army. References to Anabaptists or fanatics in religion normally come from Anglicans or Presbyterians hostile to religious toleration.

Note that the spelling of surnames was eccentric and inconsistent in the seventeenth century; names were often spelled phonetically. For example:

• Haselrige, Heselrigg, Hazelridge

- Disborowe, Desborough
- Butler, Boteler
- Monk, Monck
- Stuart, Stewart

CROMWELL BY HIS CONTEMPORARIES

Read these documents closely and complete the exercises set for each document.

Document 1
In this document Clarendon shows some balance in giving Cromwell credit for having strength of character. However, he infers that when Cromwell acts mercifully it is out of indifference rather than morality.

Exercise
Where in the document is proof of Clarendon's balance of judgement?

> For he could never have done half that mischieve without great parts of courage and industry and judgment. And he must have had a wonderful understanding in the natures and humours of men, and as great a dexterity in the applying them, who from a private and obscure birth (though of a good family), without interest of estate, alliance or friendships, could raise himself to such a height, …
> Without doubt, no man with more wickedness ever attempted any thing, or brought to pass what he desired more wickedly, more in the face and contempt of religion and moral honesty; yet wickedness as great as his could never have accomplished those trophies without the assistance of a great spirit, an admirable circumspection and sagacity, and a most magnanimous resolution …
>
> He was not a man of blood, and totally declined Machiavelli's method, which prescribes upon any alteration of a government, as a thing absolutely necessary, to cut off all the heads of those, and extirpate their families, who are friends to the old [one]. And it was confidently reported, that in the Council of Officers it was more than once proposed that there might be a general massacre of all the royal party, as the only expedient to secure the government, but Cromwell would never consent to it; it may be, out of too much contempt of his enemies. In a word, as he had all the wickedness against which damnation is denounced and for which hell-fire is prepared, so he had some virtues which have caused the memory of some men in all ages to be celebrated; and he will be looked upon by posterity as a brave bad man.

(Clarendon, *History of the Great Rebellion*, ed. Macray, 1992, vol. 15, pp. 91–7)

Document 2

Baxter, in this extract, shows his Presbyterian bias but at the same time gives Cromwell some credit for wishing to do good. However, for Baxter, Cromwell is ambitious and self-seeking.

Exercise

Where is the evidence in this document for Baxter's Presbyterian bias? How does Baxter suggest that Cromwell is ambitious?

Never man was highlier extolled, and never man was baselier reported of and vilified than this man. No (mere) man was *better* and *worse* spoken of than he, according as men's interests led their judgments. The soldiers and sectaries most highly magnified him till he began to seek the crown and the establishment of his family. And then there were so many that would be half-kings themselves that a king did seem intolerable to them. The Royalists abhorred him as a most perfidious hypocrite, and the Presbyterians thought him little better in his management of public matters.

If after so many others I may speak my opinion of him, I think that, having been prodigal in his youth and afterward changed to a zealous religiousness, he meant honestly in the main, and was pious and conscionable in the main course of his life till prosperity and success corrupted him; ...

He seemed exceeding open-hearted, by a familiar rustic-affected carriage (especially to his soldiers in sporting with them); but he thought secrecy a virtue and dissimulation no vice, ... – that is, in plain English, a lie – or perfidiousness to be a tolerable fault in a case of necessity; being of the same opinion with the Lord Bacon that 'the best composition and temperature is to have openness in fame and opinion, secrecy in habit, dissimulation in seasonable use, and a power to feign if there be no remedy' (Essay vi. p. 31). Therefore he kept fair with all, saving his open or unreconcilable enemies. He carried with it such dissimulation that Anabaptists, Independents and Antinomians did all think that he was one of them. But he never endeavoured to persuade the Presbyterians that he was one of them, but only that he would do them justice and preserve them, and that he honoured their worth and piety; for he knew that they were not so easily deceived. He meaneth well in all this at the beginning, and thinketh he doth all for the safety of the godly and the public good, but not without an eye to himself.

(Baxter, 1696, *The Autobiography of Richard Baxter*, ed. Keeble, 1974, pp. 85–9)

Document 3

Slingsby Bethel is the most hostile, seeing Cromwell as an arch schemer playing off one side against the other.

Exercise

Where is the proof in this document of Bethel's hostility?

[Cromwell's] want of honour, so well as honesty, appears yet further in that having, by a long series of seeming pious deportment, gained by his dissimulation good thoughts in his masters, the Long Parliament, and by his spiritual gifts winded [i.e. wound] himself into so good an opinion with his soldiers ... that he could impose ... what belief he pleased upon them, he made use of the credit he had with each to abuse both, by many vile practices, for making himself popular, and the Parliament and army odious to one another; and because the artifices he used are too many to innumerate, I shall but instance [a] few, [such] as ... his obstructing the House in their business by long drawling speeches and other ways, and then complaining of them to his soldiers that he could not get them to do anything that was good; his giving fair words to everyone, without keeping promise with any except for his own advantage ... and his deserting the major-generals ... crying out against them himself when he only had set them at work ... What he did ... being for his own singular advancement ... is unpardonable, and leaves him a person to be truly admired for nothing but apostasy and ambition.

(Bethel, *The World's Mistake in Oliver Cromwell*, 1972, pp. 15–16)

Document 4

For Lucy Hutchinson, Cromwell is in essence a military dictator.

Exercise

How does Hutchinson suggest that Cromwell is a military dictator?

Cromwell and his army grew wanton with their power, and invented a thousand tricks of government which, when nobody opposed, they themselves fell to dislike and vary every day ... He makes up several sorts of mock parliaments, but not finding one of them absolutely for his turn, turned them off again ... True religion was now almost lost, even among the religious party, and hypocrisy became an epidemical disease ... He at last exercised such an arbitrary power that the whole land grew weary of him.

(*Memoirs of the Life of Colonel Hutchinson*, written by his widow Lucy, ed. N.H. Keeble, 2000, pp. 293–4)

Document 5

Bishop Burnet is a Whig, which means that he has little sympathy for absolute monarchy. He sees Cromwell as being divided between religious enthusiasm and political expediency in a way that some modern historians have. In some ways this is the most balanced assessment.

Exercise

In what ways can we prove the assertion that Burnet is balanced in his judgement?

> I thought a just account of him, which I had from sure hands, might be no unacceptable thing. He never could shake off the roughness of his education and temper; he always spoke long and very ungracefully. The [religious] enthusiast and the dissembler mixed so equally … that it was not easy to tell which was the prevailing character. He was indeed both … he thought moral laws were only binding on ordinary occasions but that on extraordinary ones these might be superseded. When his own designs did not lead him out of the way, he was a lover of justice and virtue, and even of learning, … he studied to seek out able and honest men and to employ them.

(Burnet, *History of His Own Time*, 1724, p. 79)

Documents 6 and 7

The following two extracts are examples of pamphlet literature designed for a mass audience with little attempt at balance and simplistic in assumptions. Their bias is obvious.

Exercise

Summarise the views in these two sources.

> He constantly stood firm and trusty in upholding the … religion, the laws of the land and the liberties of his country, even to the very [end] of his days, and in a most devout profession and defending of them altogether, with the privileges of Parliament, of the breach of which, none was more tender and fought more valiantly for their preservation.

(*An Exact Character or Narrative of the late Right Noble and Magnificent Oliver Cromwell*, 1658)

> He cares not to spill the blood of his subjects like water plenty whereof was shed in our streets, during his short and troublesome reign, by his oppression, dissimulation, hypocrises and cruelty.

(G. Bate, *The Lives, Actions and Execution of the Prime Contrivers of that Horrid Murder of our Late Pious and Sacred Sovereign*, 1661)

The first accounts of Cromwell dating from after the Restoration are almost uniformly hostile. This is not surprising; the Restoration meant another upheaval in people's lives, and many of the political nation had fought against Charles' father and were now anxious to establish themselves with the new regime. They tried to give the impression of having only reluctantly co-operated with Cromwell and of being always secretly anxious for the glorious restoration of their rightful king. This is a familiar theme throughout history: the previous regime is damned and, if a scapegoat can be found, so much the better. It cannot be said that this applies to **Clarendon**: he was a Royalist from 1641, and his hostility to Cromwell is predictable and understandable.

By the nineteenth century Cromwell was being reassessed. This was largely not because of any new evidence, but because of a changed political climate. In the nineteenth century Whig and later Liberal politicians believed in freedom of speech, freedom of conscience and the gradual extension of the vote. They were hostile to any monarchical power (as opposed to having a 'constitutional monarch' with no real powers as a convenient figure head), and therefore the events of 1640–60 seemed to be part of the progress towards these goals that they all believed was the 'meaning' of English history. With their very Victorian belief in progress and history as progress, Cromwell was not a tyrannical regicide, but a forward-looking progressive faced with an out-dated, devious absolutist. **Thomas Macaulay**'s *History of England* (1702) was perhaps the first to describe some merit in Cromwell. **Thomas Carlyle**, a historian who believed that 'all history is the history of great men', in the middle of the century, effectively resurrected Cromwell's reputation by publishing a heavily edited, but valuable edition of his letters and speeches.

By 1900, with biographies by Whig historians such as **C. A. Firth**, and the monumental and meticulously researched *History of the Great Civil War* by **S. R. Gardiner** (continued to 1658 by Firth), Cromwell was seen as a man of virtues, such as courage, toleration and principle as well as a military genius. However, both Gardiner and Firth, despite their scholarship, saw him through the eyes of nineteenth century liberalism; a great influence on the extension of liberty of the individual and an opponent of divine right monarchy, which they, of course, deplored.

Modern historians have been divided about Cromwell. Conservatives such as **J. P. Kenyon** have seen him as a failure with essentially a negative career, able to destroy but not build: 'single-handed he postponed the inevitable restoration of the monarchy for [ten years] … his increasing authoritarianism … weakened the cause for which he had struggled'. Another conservative, **H. R. Trevor-Roper**, describes his authoritarian failure, unable to control his Parliament: 'on a superficial level Cromwell was as great an enemy of Parliament as ever Charles I ... had been, the only difference being that, as an enemy, he was more successful: he scattered his parliaments and died in his bed'.

From a very different political perspective **Christopher Hill**, in his stimulating biography *God's Englishman* (1972), also sees Cromwell as, in some ways a failure. Hill sees Cromwell as a heroic figure in the 1640s, who eventually had to hold a divided nation together, becoming increasingly conservative and seeing himself in his own words as 'the good constable of the parish', but whose power in the last resort 'rested on bayonets'. For Hill the turning point in Cromwell's career was his rejection of the 'radicals' after 1649.

In *The Lord Protector* (1955), **R. S. Paul** stresses Cromwell's desire for religious toleration and his consistency in trying to achieve it; he absolves Cromwell from the charge of personal ambition.

In *The Rump Parliament* (1974) and in later work, **Blair Worden** considers Cromwell as an 'ideological schizophrenic', torn between his instincts as a conservative country gentleman and the role he assumed in the 1640s, and his independency and sense of moral mission. This meant that during the 1650s he veered between 'healing and settling' and drastic reformation.

Derek Hirst also sees Cromwell as divided in his mind between conservatism and godly reformation, but stresses that his relationship with the army was not only politically but also emotionally important to him.

Barry Coward takes the view that, in the last analysis, it was religion that drove Cromwell – his desire to create a godly society. His actions can be explained by his religious fervour and his belief in his relationship with God.

Peter Gaunt stresses his tolerance and his desire to work through institutions, making the point that he moved into the background and let the Council take very important decisions.

John Morrill has written extensively on Cromwell and in some ways can be seen as one of the best informed of commentators. He sees Cromwell's religious conversion and the experience of being in financial difficulties in the late 1620s and early 1630s as crucial to understanding his worldview.

Ronald Hutton has been more hostile to Cromwell than most modern historians. He sees the Protectorate as a sterile failure and suggests that

Cromwell was not just driven by religion and principle. Hutton takes the view that Cromwell often acted in his own interests and could be devious.

Austin Woolrych, on the other hand, suggests that Cromwell's problems were a result of trying to create both a 'godly reformation' and a political settlement acceptable to the majority of the gentry. To Woolrych, Cromwell is not a reactionary military dictator and hypocrite, but an idealist struggling with an almost impossible situation. He sees his rule as more tolerant than that of the Rump, and his control of the army actually preventing a military dictatorship.

EXAMPLES OF HISTORIANS' VIEWS OF CROMWELL

Exercise
Read through the following extracts. They are the views of different historians. Summarise the view of each historian about Cromwell. This can be done in discussion or as a written assignment.

Document 8
This attachment to parliaments in principle also explains Cromwell's underlying respect for constitutional propriety. He made great play of the fact that he always allowed his parliaments to deliberate free from Protectoral interference; and throughout his career he carefully distanced himself from the more flagrant breaches of parliamentary privilege, such as Pride's Purge or the exclusion of elected members from both the first and second Protectorate Parliaments. Although Cromwell probably approved of the motives which lay behind these episodes, he apparently did not wish to be associated with unconstitutional purges of parliament. When the interests of the godly and the interests of the nation, or of a national institution, came into collision, Cromwell usually drew back, waited and reflected.

This trait was symptomatic of a profound ambiguity at the very core of Cromwell's personality. His speeches to successive parliaments never quite resolved one pivotal issue: who were members representative of and responsible to, 'the people of God' or 'the people' as a whole? He hoped that ultimately these two interests would be reconciled; that the entire nation could be turned towards the ways of godliness; and that parliament would play a crucial role in leading this process of spiritual regeneration.

(David L. Smith, *Cromwelliana*, 1995)

Document 9

If we emphasize the 1640s we can with Marvell see Oliver Cromwell
as 'the force of angry heaven's flame', and elemental power cleaving its
way through all opposition

> To ruin the great work of time,
> And cast the kingdom old
> Into another mould,

Or we can see him as the fiery protagonist of greater liberty of
thought and opportunity, hostile to dogmatism, privilege and shams.
If on the other hand we dwell on Cromwell's suppression of the
Levellers and his subsequent uneasy career, he appears an all-too-
human class-conscious conservative, a wily politician using all his arts
to preserve a hated military regime – and as the founder of the British
Empire. We can no doubt find threads of continuity in Oliver's
personality, his religion, his social prejudices ... I sympathise with the
ageing, disillusioned man who struggled on under the burden of the
protectorate, knowing that without him worse would befall: who
wanted to be painted 'warts and all'. But it is the boisterous and
confident leader of the 1640s who holds my imagination, and whose
pungent, earthy truths echo down the centuries. So long as men and
women 'with the root of the matter in them' call in question those
values of their society which deny our common humanity, so long
indeed as the great issues of liberty and equality which Oliver raised
remain unresolved, so long will he continue to fascinate, and the
debate over him will continue.

(Christopher Hill, *God's Englishman*, 1972)

Document 10

The great Protector had never been a statesman. Throughout his
career the main political initiatives had been created, the constitution
drawn up by others. His genius had been to execute them, and to
inspire those involved in the process. Once everybody else was out of
ideas, Cromwell was the last man to provide any ... In many ways his
tale, like that of his great opponent Charles I, had been a tragedy.
Both men had sincerely wished the best for their country and viewed
all of their actions to which others took exception as necessities.
Cromwell certainly may be credited with more ability to distinguish
between his country and himself and to recognise that the necessities
might be regrettable.

(Ronald Hutton, *The British Republic*, 2000)

Document 11

A (perhaps the) major reason for the trouble Cromwell had with Protectorate parliaments was the fear and hatred some MPs had of the army. Yet Cromwell's failures to achieve his most deeply held aims are not explicable solely in terms of the paranoid fears of gentry, lawyers and orthodox ministers. Cromwell himself contributed directly to his own failure. Cromwell was, at times, much more ruthless and more willing to disregard civil rights and postpone meetings of 'free' parliaments than has often been realised and that he never abandoned his commitment to his vision of godly reformation. Yet he was no archetypal military dictator. He punctuated periods of authoritarian rule with attempts at 'healing and settling', when he paid more attention to cultivating conservative support for the regime than promoting reformation.

(Barry Coward, *Oliver Cromwell*, 1991)

Document 12

Most modern historians and biographers have seized on the conflict between his conservative, traditional instincts and inclinations and his commitment to the army and the Puritan sects. And it is often implied that the Protectorate was therefore inherently unstable and impermanent. This of course is said with the advantage of hindsight. If Cromwell had lived ten, or even five, years longer, if he had had a more adequate successor (both of which are logical possibilities), then it might all look very different. As to the quality of the regime, the Protectorate achieved more by way of limited, practical reform than the Commonwealth had done; and the leadership was less self-indulgent. It was no more harsh than most other governments of its time. Revolutionary regimes which fail to gain *de jure* recognition are inherently more likely to be forced into taking repressive measures. But, as Clarendon tacitly conceded, Cromwell was not inhumane or bloodthirsty enough to pursue a policy of mass liquidation. And, in so far as unregenerate royalists were members of the traditional ruling class of peers and upper gentry, his object was to convert, or at least to conciliate, rather than to destroy them. Only convicted conspirators were executed. For the mass of the population, too, the Protectorate was certainly no worse than most other governments, arguably better than many. Its most damaging feature arose from excessive military and naval expenditure, although even in taxation there was some amelioration by comparison with the years 1642–53. A description of the Protectorate as a mere military dictatorship is inadequate; the rule of Oliver Cromwell was both more and less than that.

(G. E. Aylmer, *Rebellion or Revolution?*, 1986)

Document 13

To see Cromwell's career as the ruthless pursuit of one goal is to give it a consistency and predictability which it lacked. Cromwell was pulled by contrary impulses. He disliked political change and feared social upheaval, and yet he had intense fellow-feeling for his soldiers and their sacrifices, believed that religious freedom must be preserved and that England had been chosen by God as the first place where the Saints would rule and give an example to the world. Often he was indecisive. Crucial decisions were left to others. He was also open-minded, willing to use schemes and supporters regardless of their origins. But on occasion he could act quickly, when army discipline faltered, when invasion threatened or when godly men were persecuted. His reluctance to rule and his lack of ambition for his sons were genuine. Yet he discovered no alternative to governing himself or to bequeathing power to his son. He hoped to preserve or revive admired institutions. He wanted to rule with a freely elected Parliament; he wanted to involve more of the propertied in local affairs. Yet he had acquiesced in the abolition of monarchy and baulked at reviving it. He faced a succession of quarrelsome Parliaments which he purged or peremptorily dismissed, and persuaded only a small fragment of the old ruling classes to re-enter office. He supported the efforts of the godly to hasten moral regeneration. As a consequence he wavered between courses little better than godly tyranny and those which deferred, almost cravenly, to the respectable. Awkwardly, he wanted to combine support from Calvinist zealots with backing from the gentry and merchants, only to discover that he was suspected by both groups. Although Cromwell denied it, most contemporaries remembered that he had been brought to power by the army and thought that his rule continued thanks to the soldier's support or forbearance.

Cromwell found high office uncongenial, yet ruled with sober dignity. If he retreated from some of his early reforming ideals, he continued to preside over a regime which was feared for its military efficiency, which kept the peace, and which was respected for its willingness to seek solutions to the intractable political, social and religious problems of the day. England had been, and would be, worse governed than it was in the 1650s.

(Toby Barnard, *The English Republic 1649–1660*, 1982)

Document 14

Yet he was never disposed to eliminate the army from politics altogether, even if he could safely have done so, because he clung to so many of the values for which it stood in the heyday of the New Model.

There lies the second major tension that strained the Protectorate. His later speeches are full of his desire to balance civil and Christian liberty, and to reconcile what he called the interest of the nation with the more particular interest of the people of God. By the interest of the nation he meant the rights and desires and susceptibilities of the unregenerate majority, and especially those of the gentry magistracy. The interest of the people of God, on the other hand, demanded the enforcement by public authority of a strict moral code and the sanctity of the Sabbath, plus the toleration of a range of sects and religious practices that to traditionalists seemed downright heretical. To a puritan of Cromwell's stamp the people of God came first, and it may be that lingering misgivings about the legitimacy of his authority were a spur to his promotion of their interests, to whose defence he thought that providence had called him. But he would never acknowledge that the two interests were necessarily in conflict. 'He sings sweetly that sings a song of reconciliation betwixt these two interest', he said, 'and it is a pitiful fancy, and wild and ignorant, to think they are inconsistent.' And again: 'If anyone whatsoever think the Interest of Christians and the Interest of the Nation inconsistent, I wish my soul may never enter into his or their secrets!' But in a wicked world they did not consist all that easily. I suggested earlier that whether the Protectorate was a dictatorship and whether it was a military dictatorship are partially separable questions. The conclusion I offer is that what there was of the dictatorial in Cromwell's rule – and there was such an element, often though it has been overstated – stemmed not so much from its military origins or the participation of army officers in civil government as from his constant commitment to the interest of the people of God, and his conviction that suppressing vice and encouraging virtue constituted 'the very end of magistracy'.

(Austin Woolrych, 'The Cromwellian Protectorate: A Military Dictatorship?', *History*, 244, June 1990)

THE CONSTITUTIONS

Constitutions are some of the hardest sources to understand. It might be a good idea to read them in a group by dividing them up into sections.

Exercise
Decide what are the main features of each constitution.

Document 15: The Instrument of Government, 1653
The government of the Commonwealth of England, Scotland and Ireland, and the dominions thereunto belonging [16 December 1653]

That the supreme legislative authority of the Commonwealth of England …[etc.] shall be and reside in one person, and the people assembled in parliament; the style of which person shall be, 'The Lord Protector of the Commonwealth of England, Scotland and Ireland.'

That the exercise of the chief magistracy, and the administration of the government over the said countries and dominions, and the people thereof, shall be in the Lord Protector, assisted with a Council, the number whereof shall not exceed twenty-one nor be less than thirteen.

That all writs, process[es], commissions, patents, grants and other things, which now run in the name and style of the Keepers of the Liberties of England by Authority of Parliament, shall run in the name and style of the Lord Protector, from whom for the future shall be derived all magistracy and honours in these three nations; and [he] shall have the power of pardons (except in case of murders and treason) and benefit of all forfeitures for the public use; and shall govern the said countries and dominions in all things by the advice of the Council, and according to these presents, and the laws.

That the Lord Protector, the parliament sitting, shall dispose and order the militia and forces, both by sea and land, for the peace and good of the three nations, by consent of parliament; and that the Lord Protector, with the advice and consent of the major part of the Council, shall dispose and order the militia for the ends aforesaid in the intervals of parliament.

That the Lord Protector, by the advice aforesaid, shall direct in all things concerning the keeping and holding of a good correspondency with foreign kings, princes and states; and also, with the consent of the major part of the Council, have the power of war and peace.

That the laws shall not be altered, suspended, abrogated, or repealed, nor any new law made, nor any tax, charge or imposition laid upon the people, but by common consent in parliament (save only as is expressed in the 30th article).

That there shall be a parliament summoned to meet at Westminster upon the third day of September, 1654, and that successively a parliament shall be summoned once in every third year, to be accounted from the dissolution of the present parliament [of 1654].

That neither the parliament to be next summoned, nor any successive parliaments, shall during the time of five months, to be accounted from the day of their first meeting, be adjourned, prorogued or dissolved, without their own consent …

That the Lord Protector, with the advice of the major part of the Council, shall at any other time than is before expressed, when the necessities of the state shall require it, summon parliaments in manner before expressed, which shall not be adjourned, prorogued, or dissolved without their own consent during the first three months of their sitting; and in case of future war with any foreign state a parliament shall be forthwith summoned for their advice concerning the same.

That all bills agreed unto by the parliament shall be presented to the Lord Protector for his consent, and in case he shall not give his consent thereto within twenty days after they shall be presented to him, or give satisfaction to the parliament within the time limited, that then upon declaration of the parliament that the Lord Protector hath not consented nor given satisfaction, such bills shall pass into and become law, although he shall not give his consent thereunto; provided such bills contain nothing in them contrary to the matters contained in these presents.

That [fourteen persons named] or any seven of them, shall be a Council for the purposes expressed in this writing and upon the death or other removal of any of them the parliament shall nominate six persons of ability, integrity, and fearing God, for every one that is dead or removed; out of which the major part of the Council shall elect two and present them to the Lord Protector, of which he shall elect one. And in case the parliament shall not nominate within twenty days after notice given unto them thereof, the major part of the Council shall nominate three as aforesaid to the Lord Protector, who out of them shall supply the vacancy. ...

That the raising of money for defraying and charge of the present extraordinary forces, both at sea and land in respect of the present wars, shall be by consent of parliament and not otherwise; save only that the Lord Protector, with the consent of the major part of the Council, for preventing the disorders and dangers which might otherwise fall out both by sea and land, shall have power, until the meeting of the first parliament, to raise money for the purposes aforesaid; and also to make laws and ordinances for the peace and welfare of these nations, where it shall be necessary, which shall be binding and in force until order shall be taken in parliament concerning the same.

That the lands, tenements, rents, royalties, jurisdictions and hereditaments which remain yet unsold or undisposed of by act or ordinance of parliament, belonging to the Commonwealth ... shall be vested in the Lord Protector to hold, to him and his successors Lords

Protectors of these nations, and shall not be alienated but by consent in parliament.

That Oliver Cromwell, Captain General, ... shall be, and is hereby declared to be, Lord Protector. ...

That the chancellor, keeper or commissioners of the Great Seal, the treasurer, admiral, chief governors of Ireland and Scotland, and the chief justices of both the Benches, shall be chosen by the approbation of parliament, and in the intervals of parliament by the approbation of the major part of the Council, to be afterwards approved by the Parliament.

(J. P. Kenyon (ed.), *The Stuart Constitution*, 1986, pp. 308–11)

Document 16: The Humble Petition and Advice, 25 May 1657

To his Highness the Lord Protector. ...

We, the knights, citizens and burgesses in this present parliament assembled ... have just judged it a duty incumbent upon on to present and declare these our most just and necessary desires to your Highness.

That your Highness will be pleased, by and under the name and style of Lord Protector of the Commonwealth of England, Scotland and Ireland, and the dominions and territories thereunto belonging, to hold and exercise the office of chief magistrate of these nations. ... That your Highness will be pleased during your lifetime to appoint and declare the person who shall immediately after your death succeed you in the government of these nations.

That your Highness will for the future be pleased to call parliaments consisting of two Houses ... once in three years at furthest, or oftener, as the affairs of the nations shall require ...

That ... those persons who are legally chosen by a free election of the people to serve in parliament may not be excluded from sitting in parliament to do their duties, but by judgment and consent of that House whereof they are members.

[Concerns those debarred from voting and being elected to parliament.]

That your Highness will consent that none be called to sit and vote in the Other House but such as are not disabled ... being such as shall be nominated by your Highness and approved by this House ...

That in all other particulars which concern the calling and holding of parliaments, your Highness will be pleased that the laws and statues of the land be observed and kept, and that no laws be altered, suspended, abrogated or repealed, or new law made, but by act of parliament.

And to the end there may be a constant revenue for support of the government, and for the safety and defence of these nations by sea and land, we declare our willingness to settle forthwith a yearly revenue of £1,300,000, whereof £1,000,000 for the navy and army, and £300,000 for the support of the government, and no part thereof to be raised by a land-tax, and this not be altered without the consent; of the three estates in parliament ... and do pray your Highness that it be enacted and declared that no charge be laid, nor person be compelled to contribute to any gift, loan, benevolence, tax, tallage, aid or any other like charge, without common consent by act of parliament, which is a freedom the people of these nations ought by the laws to inherit.

That none may be admitted to the Privy Council of your Highness or successors, but such as are of known piety and undoubted affection to the rights of these nations, and a just Christian liberty in matters of religion, nor without consent of the Council to be afterwards approved by both Houses of Parliament, and shall not afterwards be removed but by consent of parliament, but may in the intervals of parliament be suspended from the exercise of his place by your Highness, by your successors and the Council, for just cause ... And that the standing forces of this Commonwealth shall be disposed of by the chief magistrate by the consent of both Houses of Parliament, the parliament sitting, and in the intervals of parliament by the chief magistrate by the advice of the Council; and also that your Highness and successors will be pleased to exercise your government over these nations by the advice of your Council.

And that the chancellor, keeper or commissioners of the Great Seal of England, the treasurer, or commissioners of the treasury, the admiral ... the chief justices of both the Benches, and the chief baron ... [and certain officers in Scotland and Ireland] shall be approved by both Houses of Parliament.

And whereas your Highness, out of your zeal to the glory of God and the propagation of the gospel of the Lord Jesus Christ, hath been pleased to encourage a godly ministry in these nations, we earnestly desire that such as do openly revile them or their assemblies, or disturb them in the worship and service of God, to the dishonour of God, scandal of good men, or breach of the peace, may be punished according to law, and where the laws are defective, that your Highness will give consent to such laws as shall be made in that behalf.

That the true Protestant Christian religion, as it is contained in the holy scriptures of the Old and New Testament, and no other, be held forth and asserted for the public profession of these nations; and that a confession of faith, to be agreed by your Highness and the Parliament, according to the rule and warrant of the scriptures, be asserted, held forth and recommended to the people of these nations, that none may be suffered or permitted by opprobrious words or writing maliciously or contemptuously to revile or reproach the Confession of Faith to be agreed upon as aforesaid. And such who profess faith in [the Trinity and acknowledge the scriptures as the word of God] and shall in other things differ in doctrine, worship or discipline from the public profession held forth, endeavours shall be used to convince them by sound doctrine and the example of a good conversation, but they may not be compelled thereto by penalties, nor restrained from their profession, but protected from all injury and molestation in the profession of the faith, and exercise of their religion, whilst they abuse not this liberty to the civil injury of others or the disturbance of the public peace; so that this liberty be not extended to popery and prelacy, or to the countenancing such who publish horrid blasphemies, or practise to hold forth licentiousness or profaneness under the profession of Christ. ...

(J. P. Kenyon (ed.), *The Stuart Constitution*, 1986, pp. 324–9)

CROMWELL'S SPEECHES

Many of Cromwell's most important pronouncements were made in Parliament. However, some of his speeches to groups such as the army survive.

Exercise
Read the speeches of Cromwell and then discuss what kind of person comes across.

Document 17: Speech to the Parliament, 12 September 1654
In this extract, Cromwell is making it clear to the Protectorate Parliament that, although they are a free Parliament, they have to accept the Instrument. He also wishes to clear himself of any charge of personal ambition, emphasising that he could have made himself much more powerful.

I did acquaint you what the first rise was of this government which hath called you hither, and in the authority of which you came hither.

Among other things that I told you of them, I said you were a free Parliament. And so you are, whilst you own the government and authority that called you hither. ... But I see it will be necessary for me now a little to magnify my office, which I have not been apt to do. I have been of this mind, I have always been of this mind, since first I entered upon it unto it, which in modesty I have hitherto forborne, I am in some measure now necessitated thereunto. And therefore that will be the prologue to my discourse.

I called not myself to this place. I say again, I called not myself to this place; of that, God is witness. ...

To make plain and clear that which I have said, I must take liberty to look back. I was by birth a gentleman, living neither in any considerable height, nor yet in obscurity. I have been called to several employments in the nation, – to serve in Parliaments, – and (because I would not be over tedious) I did endeavour to discharge the duty of an honest man in those services, to God, and his people's interest, and of the Commonwealth; having, when time was, a competent acceptation in the hearts of men, and some evidences thereof. I resolve not to recite the times and occasions, and opportunities that have been appointed me by God to serve him, nor the presence and blessings of God bearing then testimony to me. I, having had some occasions to see, together with my brethren and countrymen, a happy period put to our sharp wars and contests with the then common enemy, hoped, in a private capacity, to have reaped the fruit and benefit, together with my brethren, of our hard labours and hazards, to wit, the enjoyment of peace and liberty, and the privileges of a Christian and of a man, in some equality with others, according as it should please the Lord to dispense unto me. ...

And I have many witnesses, who I do believe could readily lay down their lives to bear witness to the truth of that, that is to say, that I called not myself to this place. And being in it, I bear not witness myself; but God and the people of these nations have borne testimony to it also. If my calling be from God, and my testimony from the people, God and the people shall take it from me, else I will not part with it. I should be false to the trust that God hath placed upon me, and to the interest of the people of these nations, if I should. ...

[After the dismissal of the Rump]

I say, the authority I had in my hand being so boundless as it was, I being by Act of Parliament General of all the forces in the three nations of England, Scotland and Ireland, – in which unlimited condition I did not desire to live a day, – did call that meeting for the ends before expressed. What the event and issue of that meeting was, we may sadly remember: it hath much teaching in it, and I hope will make us all wiser for the future. But this meeting succeeding, as I have formerly said to you, and giving such a disappointment of our hopes, I shall not now make any repetition thereof. Only the effect was, that they came and brought to me a parchment, signed by very much the major part of them, expressing their resigning and redelivery of the power and authority that was committed to them back again into my hands. And I can say it in the presence of divers persons here, that do know whether I lie in that, that I did not know one tittle of that resignation, until they all came and brought it, and delivered it into my hands; of this there are also in this presence many witnesses. I received this resignation, having formerly used my endeavours and persuasions to keep them together ... They told me that except I would undertake the government ... blood and confusion would break in on us ... I confess after many arguments, and after the letting me know that I did not receive anything that did not put me into any higher capacity than I was in before, but that it limited me and bound my hands to act nothing to the prejudice of the nations without consent of a council until the parliament met, and then limited me by the Parliament as the Act of Government expresseth, I did accept it.

(I. Roots (ed.), *The Speeches of Oliver Cromwell*, 1989)

Document 18: Cromwell's speech to 100 officers of the army, regarding the offer of kingship, March 1657
In the account of this speech, Cromwell berates the officers for interfering in politics and infers that he has done much for them.

I suppose you have heard of the address made by one hundred officers to his Highness yesterday seven-night, that his Highness would not hearken to the title [of king] because it was not pleasing to his army and was matter of scandal to the people of God, of great rejoicing to the enemy; that it was hazardous to his own person and of great danger to the three nations; such an assumption making way for Charles Stuart to come in again.

His Highness returned answer presently to this effect, That the first man that told him of it was he, the mouth of his officers then present, (meaning Colonel Mills); that for his part he had never been at any cabal about the same, (hinting by that the frequent cabals that were against kingship by certain officers).

He said the time was when they boggled not at the word (king), for the Instrument by which the government now stands was presented to his Highness with the title (king) in it, as some there present could witness, (pointing at a principal officer then in his eye,) and he refused to accept of the title. But how it comes to pass that they now startle at that title, they best knew. That for his part he loved not the title, a feather in a hat, as little as they did.

That they had made him their drudge upon all occasions. To dissolve the Long Parliament, who had contracted evil enough by long sitting. To call a parliament, or Convention, of their naming; who met, and what did they? Fly at liberty and property, in so much as if one man had twelve cows, they held another that wanted cows ought to take a share with his neighbour. Who could have said anything was their own, if they had gone on? After their dissolution, how was I pressed by you (said he) for the rooting out of the ministry, nay rather than fail, to starve them out!

A parliament was afterwards called; they sat five months; it's true we hardly heard of them in all that time. They took the Instrument into debate, and they must needs be dissolved; and yet stood not the Instrument in need of mending? Was not the case hard with me, to be put upon to swear to that which was hard to be kept?

Some time after that, you thought it was necessary to have major-generals, and the first rise to that motion then was the late general insurrections, and was justifiable, and your major-generals did your parts well; you might have gone on. Who bid you go to the House with a Bill and there receive a foil?

After you had exercised this power a while, impatient were you till a parliament was called. I gave my vote against it, but you were confident by your own strength and interest to get men chosen to your hearts and desires. How you have failed therein and how much the country hath been disobliged is well known.

That it is time to come to a settlement, and lay aside arbitrary proceedings so unacceptable to the nation. And by the proceedings of this Parliament you see they stand in need of a check or balancing power, (meaning the House of Lords, or a house so constituted) for the case of James Naylor might happen to be your own case. By their judicial power they fall upon life and member, and doth the Instrument in being enable me to control it?

These were some of the heads insisted on in his speech, though perhaps not the same words yet the full sense and the officers since that time are quieted.

(I. Roots (ed.), *The Speeches of Oliver Cromwell*, 1989)

Document 19: Cromwell declines the Crown, April–May 1657

In these speeches Cromwell rejects kingship on the grounds that it is unnecessary and that many people would object to him being king. He also argues that kingship has been destroyed by God's providence and cast out by an Act of Parliament.

Truly though kingship be not a title, but a name of office that runs through the law. It is a name of office plainly implying the supreme authority; it is no more, nor can it be stretched to more ... signification goes to the thing and not to the name ... Why then there can be no more said but this. Why, this hath been said, this hath been the name fixed, under which the supreme authority has been known. Happily as it hath been fixed, so it may be unfixed ... And if it be so that you may, why then, I say there is nothing of necessity in the argument, but consideration of the expedience of it ... I say undoubtedly, let us think what we will, what the Parliament settles is that which will run through the law, and will lead the thread of government through the land ... consent of the whole will, I say, be the needle that will lead the thread through all, and I think no man will pretend right against it or wrong. And if so, then, under favour to me, I think all those arguments from the law are, as I said before, not necessary, but are to be understood upon the account of conveniency ...

... truly I should have urged one consideration more that I had forgotten; and that is, not only to urge from reason but from experience ... the supreme authority going in another name and under another title than king, why it has been complied with twice without it ... And truly I may say that almost universal obedience has been given from all ranks and sort of men to both ... And therefore I say, (under favour) these two experiences do manifestly show, that it is not a title, though so interwoven with the laws, that makes the law to have its free passage and do its office without interruption (as we think) but that if a parliament shall determine that another name shall run through the laws, I believe it may run with as free a passage as this ...

(W. C. Abbott, *Writings and Speeches of Cromwell*, 1937, vol. 4, pp. 445–6, speech to Lord Whitelocke and the Commons Committee, 3 April 1657)

I think from my very heart that in your settling of the peace and liberties of this nation, which cried as loud upon you as ever nation did, [you should labour] for somewhat that may beget a consistency, otherwise the nation will fall to pieces. And in that, as far as I can, I am ready to serve not as a king, but as a constable ...

I tell you there are such men in this nation that are godly, men of the same spirit, men that will not be beaten down with a carnal or worldly spirit while they keep their integrity. I deal plainly and faithfully with you, I cannot think that God would bless me in the undertaking of anything that would justly and with cause grieve them ... Truly the providence of God has laid this title aside providentially. *De facto* it is laid as aside and this not by sudden humour or passion; but it has been the issue of ten or twelve years' civil war, wherein much blood has been shed ... And God has seemed providentially not only to strike at the family but at the name. And as I said before, *de facto* it is blotted out, it is a thing cast out by Act of Parliament, it's a thing has been kept out to this day ... I would not seek to set up that that providence hath destroyed and laid in the dust, and I would not build Jericho again ...

(W. C. Abbott, *Writings and Speeches of Cromwell*, 1937, vol. 4, pp. 467–74, speech to the same committee, 13 April 1657)

ASSESSMENT

QUESTIONS IN THE STYLE OF EDEXCEL

Introduction

Unit 6, *The Quest for Settlement: Cromwell and the Protectorate, 1653–58*, is the synoptic unit for your examination. It is not synoptic in the sense of content, but skills. Therefore technique is of utmost importance. There are two areas to focus on:

- Analysis
- Sourcework

Both (a) and (b) questions demand that you respond in an analytical fashion. That means that you develop an argument in response to the question set. The questions are framed in such a way as to allow analysis to take place.

(a) The question asks you to *explain* a factor/issue relating to some element of the course content. However, you should not be misled: the best way to answer the question is not to write an explanation but to create an argument and to analyse. In doing so, you move automatically to the top band and are often placed at the top of that band.

A common mistake is for candidates to underestimate the importance of the (a) question. Those who achieve near full marks set themselves up for an A/B grade even with a weaker performance on the essay.

(b) The question will be framed in such a way as to facilitate a relatively straightforward argument. You will be given an interpretation or a view and be asked to what extent you agree. The answer is therefore 'up to a point … but'. It is for you to qualify the extent to which you agree.

Using the sources

The questions ask you to use the sources. In doing so you need to show evidence that you possess the following skills:

- **comprehension of evidence**: both at face value and reading between the lines;
- **provenance**: you need to show that you understand that the provenance of the evidence is an important factor to consider;
- **utility**;
- **cross-referencing**: you need to be able to treat the sources together and highlight where the sources agree and where there are significant differences. You also need to explain why there are these similarities and differences.

It is very important to note that these skills need to be performed at the level of A2 rather than AS. The main failing of so many candidates answering the A2 paper is that they answer at a basic level.

Technique

The sources must be used as part of the analytical response. Below is a suggested paragraph structure that facilitates both analysis and sourcework at a level required for full marks:

- **Argue**. At the start of the paragraph you should present a line of argument. The best way to do this is to use the language of argument:

  One should argue that …
  It is clear that …
  Fundamentally …
  Without doubt …
  This most obviously …

  Try and avoid a descriptive start because this will often lead to a descriptive paragraph.
- **Explain**. The next section of each paragraph will explain that line of argument.
- **Evidence**. The difficulty for candidates in completing their answers is that they are expected to give evidence from their own knowledge and explain the relevance of detail used to back up their argument. This detail needs to be accurate, well selected and relevant. What is meant by detail? Facts, statistics, names, events, references to historians.

You are also expected to use the sources and evaluate, criticise, cross-reference and interpret the sources as part of this process.

Reiterate. The last half sentence of the paragraph should be a reiteration, going back to the main theme/argument in the question.

Here is an example of a model paragraph showing how you might write. Once you have read this, complete the exercise.

The rule of the major-generals was perceived as harsh because it was associated with the brutal crushing of Penruddock's Rising in Wiltshire in March 1655. Indeed the major-generals' experiment that followed had the effect of creating the legend of Cromwell as a military dictator. Equally damaging were the orders received by the major-generals including banning horse races, cock fighting and stage plays. The reaction against this experiment can be seen in Source B in which the historian, well informed and reliable, attacks the major-generals as 'the most intolerable experience England ever had'. This view is complemented by that of the contemporary writing in Source C, who believed that the major-generals 'are as destructive a force as we have known'. Although one has to be aware that the contemporary is clearly an opponent of Cromwell and is writing after 1660 and will therefore invariably condemn, it is clear that he was in a position to understand the impact of the major-generals at the time. So the evidence of contemporary and historian condemn the experiment as negative.

Study Sources A–E below and then answer questions (a) and (b) which follow:

Source A

He was not a man of blood, and totally declined Machiavelli's method, which prescribes upon any alteration of a government, as a thing absolutely necessary, to cut off all the heads of those, and extirpate their families, who are friends to the old [one.] And it was confidently reported, that in the Council of Officers it was more than once proposed that there might be a general massacre of all the royal party, as the only expedient to secure the government, but Cromwell would never consent to it; it may be, out of too much contempt of his enemies. In a word, as he had all the wickedness against which damnation is denounced and for which hell-fire is prepared, so he had some virtues which have caused the memory of some men in all ages to be celebrated; and he will be looked upon by posterity as a brave bad man.

From Lord Clarendon's *History of the Great Rebellion*, written in the late 1660s.

Source B

Cromwell's talk [in the 1650s] of 'healing and settling' underpins the common assumption that the Protectorate represented an attempt to sheath the sword, which the army had turned to naked political use. Such an analysis needs to be qualified. Cromwell had always been reluctant to take the army into politics [but] sheathing the sword was not the same as laying it down. Although there were more civilians than serving officers on his Council, the dominant figure, after Cromwell himself, was the brilliant, witty, but still soldierly, John Lambert. More revealing was the situation in the localities, where Cromwell left intact the remaining garrisons which so troubled the gentry and the clergy; nor did he purge the many army officers from the ranks of JPs. He had too much to lose. Not only did the soldiers keep the royalists down; they were also his only hope of combining godly rule with godly liberty.

From Derek Hirst's *Authority and Conflict: England 1603-1658*, 1986.

Source C

Occasionally one still finds the Protectorate glibly branded as a military dictatorship, but the description is most misleading. Cromwell himself praised the constitution because it separated the legislative and executive powers, instead of leaving both under the control of a parliament that acknowledged no bounds to its authority, and because it restored the old idea of a balance in the constitution. The executive power was vested in the Protector and the Council and he was bound to govern in all things by its advice. Nor was he free to appoint or dismiss councillors at his pleasure. This restraint would have meant little if the Council had been a rubber stamp or junta of army officers, but it was neither. Its role in decision-making has been often underestimated and the military element in it exaggerated. Only four of Cromwell's fifteen original councillors belonged to the field army. Civilians outnumbered soldiers by two to one and their preponderance increased with subsequent appointments to the Council.

From Austin Woolrych's *England Without a King 1649-1660*, 1983.

Source D

I think the state to be in an extremely uncertain condition, since it appears to be based solely on force and the army, and it is more than probable that there is very little support in this country for the government. The army itself consists mainly of a collection of officers who as to the greater part of them have been drawn from the common people. The Protector's maxim seems to be that such people must stick to him since any change of regime can be expected to cause their inevitable ruin and downfall. The common soldiers he binds to himself by the high pay he gives them.

> Christian Bonde, newly-arrived Swedish ambassador to England, writing to the King of Sweden in July 1655.

Source E

A (perhaps the) major reason for the trouble Cromwell had with Protectorate parliaments was the fear and hatred some MPs had of the army. Yet Cromwell's failures to achieve his most deeply held aims are not explicable solely in terms of the paranoid fears of gentry, lawyers and orthodox ministers. Cromwell himself contributed directly to his own failure. Cromwell was, at times, much more ruthless and more willing to disregard civil rights and postpone meetings of 'free' parliaments than has often been realised and that he never abandoned his commitment to his vision of godly reformation. Yet he was no archetypal military dictator. He punctuated periods of authoritarian rule with attempts at 'healing and settling', when he paid more attention to cultivating conservative support for the regime than promoting reformation.

> From Barry Coward's *Oliver Cromwell*, 1991.

Answer both questions (a) and (b):

(a) Using your own knowledge, and the evidence of Sources A, B and E, what do you consider to have been Cromwell's main political characteristics? (10)

(b) A 'ruthless military dictatorship': Using your own knowledge, and the evidence of these sources, explain how far you would agree with this interpretation of government during the Protectorate. (20)

QUESTIONS IN THE STYLE OF OCR

The debate on the nature of Cromwell's rule

Source A

(A republican opponent of Cromwell condemns the Protector's ambition.)

Having seen our cause betrayed and the most solemn promises violated, I departed from my native country. General Cromwell had long been suspected by wise and good men; but he had taken such care to mould the army to his interests that he had filled all places either with his own creatures or with such as hoped to share with him in the sovereignty, and removed those who had the courage to oppose him. His wicked intentions were not revealed openly till after the battle at Worcester. Mr Hugh Peters said to a friend that Cromwell would make himself king. But either the General's ambition was so great that he could not resist ascending the throne until the time set by Parliament for its sitting had expired or his fear hastened him to the achievement of his plans. It is certain that he vehemently desired to be rid of this Parliament that had performed such great things.

From Edmund Ludlow's *Memoirs*, 1698.

Source B

(A Marxist historian examines Cromwell's conflicting loyalties.)

His unique prestige with the army made him the indispensable head of state so long as the army was a power in the land; his genuine desire for a parliamentary settlement continually raised hopes that he might yet square the circle. But, just because Oliver owed his position to the army, he could never in the last resort break from it. Oliver could ride the two horses, like a trick rider at the circus, though he could never transfer his weight from one to the other, and transform military rule into parliamentary government.

From Christopher Hill's *Oliver Cromwell*, 1958.

Source C

(Another historian sees the contradictions of Cromwell.)

To see Cromwell's career as the ruthless pursuit of one goal is to give it a consistency and predictability which it lacked. Cromwell was pulled by contrary impulses. He disliked political change and feared social upheaval, and yet he had intense fellow-feeling for his soldiers and their sacrifices, believed that religious freedom must be preserved and that England had been chosen by God as the first place where the Saints would rule and give an example to the world. Often he was indecisive. Crucial decisions were left to others. He was also open-minded, willing to use schemes and supporters regardless of their origins. But on occasion he could act quickly, when army discipline faltered, when invasion threatened or when godly men were persecuted. His reluctance to rule and his lack of ambition for his sons were genuine. Yet he discovered no alternative to governing himself or to bequeathing power to his son. He hoped to preserve or revive admired institutions. He wanted to rule with a freely elected Parliament; he wanted to involve more of the propertied in local affairs. Yet he had acquiesced in the abolition of monarchy and baulked at reviving it. He faced a succession of quarrelsome Parliaments which he purged or peremptorily dismissed, and persuaded only a small fragment of the old ruling classes to re-enter office. He supported the efforts of the godly to hasten moral regeneration. As a consequence he wavered between courses little better than godly tyranny and those which deferred, almost cravenly, to the respectable. Awkwardly, he wanted to combine support from Calvinist zealots with backing from the gentry and merchants, only to discover that he was suspected by both groups.

From Toby Barnard's *The English Republic 1649-1660*, 1982.

Source D
(The author of a more recent biography presents a different interpretation.)

The conclusion I offer is that what there was of the dictatorial in Cromwell's rule – and there was such an element, often though it has been overstated – stemmed not so much from its military origins or the participation of army officers in civil government as from his constant commitment to the interest of the people of God, and his conviction that suppressing vice and encouraging virtue constituted 'the very end of magistracy'.

From Austin Woolrych's *The Cromwellian Protectorate A Military Dictatorship?*, 1990.

You should answer **Question 1** and **one** other question:

> **1 (a)** How effectively does Source C deal with the suggestion that Cromwell was over ambitious made in Source A? **(15)**

How to answer this question
The question is asking you to explain and evaluate two different views. To answer this question it is very important that you:

- focus on key issues in the sources and are successful in explaining the historians' arguments;
- try to include comments on the credibility, typicality, value and usefulness of the sources;
- make use of both sources and draw comparisons between them;
- compare the content of the sources against contextual knowledge.

> **1 (b)** Using Sources A to D, explain why there is so much debate about Cromwell's motivation. **(30)**

How to answer this question
The question is asking you to evaluate the sources in the context of the different historical interpretations of Cromwell's motivation. To answer this question fully it is important that you do the following:

- make full use of all four sources, testing them against your own knowledge and evaluating their utility. This own knowledge does not have to be explained in full but used as evidence to back up the argument and evaluation;
- show that you have an understanding of the range of interpretations about what drove Cromwell;
- analyse the sources, evaluating them both individually and as a set.

> **2** How valid is the judgement that Cromwell's rule was driven by 'the ruthless pursuit of power'? **(45)**
>
> **3** To what extent were Cromwell's actions in Ireland motivated by religious zeal? **(45)**
>
> (Total: 90 marks)

How to answer these questions

In answering these questions you need to be analytical throughout. Below are a few tips on the technique necessary to write such essays. Marks are easily thrown away because your essay technique is not as strong as it should be. The aim of this section is to give you guidance on how to write an assignment that is analytical throughout. These are the main features you need to concentrate on:

- structure
- context
- directness
- evidence

Introduction. Once you have written a plan you need to write an introduction that answers the question.

- The introduction will involve writing out the main points from the plan.
- It is essential that you attack the question directly in the introduction.
- Your introduction should be straightforward, direct and deliver an answer to the question.

Paragraph structure. You need to structure your assignment into clear and sufficient paragraphs. To achieve the mark you want you need to stay direct to the argument throughout. This means that you **explicitly answer the question** throughout the essay. The best structure for every paragraph is thus:

- **Argue.** At the start of the paragraph you should present a line of argument. The best way to do this is to use the language of argument:

  One should argue that …
  It is clear that …
  Fundamentally …
  Without doubt …
  This most obviously …

  Try and avoid a descriptive start because this will often lead to a descriptive paragraph.

- **Explain.** The next section of each paragraph will explain that line of argument.

- **Evidence.** 'The clearest example of this point is the …'. The next section of the paragraph should give and explain the relevance of detail that you have used to back up your argument. This detail needs to be accurate, well selected and relevant. What is meant by detail? Facts, statistics, names, events, references to historians.

Reiterate. The last half sentence of the paragraph should be a reiteration, going back to the main theme/argument in the question.

QUESTION IN THE STYLE OF AQA

Study the sources below and answer the question that follows:

Source A

After 1653 Oliver was desperately trying to arrive at a 'settlement', some agreement with a parliament by which the army could be reduced and the burden of taxation lessened. Yet the dilemma was inescapable. Any parliament would demand the subordination of the army to itself. The dissolution of Barebones Parliament left the dictatorship of the generals naked and unashamed. The Instrument of Government spread a fig leaf over this nakedness by providing a parliamentary constitution. The Instrument also endeavoured to perpetuate the veiled dictatorship of the generals by writing into the constitution, as a first charge on revenue, an army of 30,000 men; and by nominating to the Council the generals, their friends and relations, and making it virtually impossible to remove them. Even a purged Parliament rejected this constitution. The rule of the major-generals which followed was efficient. But they encountered solid opposition from precisely those groups which Parliament represented – town oligarchies and country gentry. Hatred of standing armies became a decisive prejudice for the British ruling class.

From Christopher Hill's, *Oliver Cromwell*, 1958.

Source B

Yet the personality of Cromwell remains enigmatic and his reputation changes – as it will continue to change – with the moral and political climate of the living world …. His actions in crisis, whether on the battlefield, in Parliament or at the Council table, show a clear and bold judgement; but he was not good at analysing or presenting the reasons behind his actions. Prayer helped him towards all his considered decisions. In his years of power there is no evidence of any personal pleasure at his own greatness. Can this be taken as evidence that personal ambition was never a motive with him? I am inclined to think so. As Protector he appeared, in spite of his power at home and prestige abroad, a sad and heavily burdened man.

From C. V. Wedgwood's *Oliver Cromwell*, 1973.

Source C

The barren record of his first parliament made clear the dilemma which he faced as a ruler of Britain. He had failed to give the people 'what pleases them' by constitutional means. His reaction was to embark on an authoritarian course of 'giving the people what's good for them'. Indeed many aspects of Cromwell's rule in 1655–6 show a lack of concern for constitutional legality that gives support to those who would depict Cromwell as a military dictator. Moreover, he underwent a personal, spiritual crisis in that period which caused him to be more than ever determined to take England, via the rule of the major-generals, into the New Jerusalem. Yet, what is striking about Cromwell, is that, even when his iron-fisted authoritarianism was most prominent, he showed that he had not totally abandoned either his political Independent instincts for 'healing and settling' or his aspirations to secure broad-based support for his regime from the parliamentary classes of the country.

From Barry Coward's *Cromwell*, 1991.

1 With reference to these three sources and to your own knowledge, consider the validity of the view that during the period 1653 to 1658 Cromwell was a willing dictator.

How to answer this question
Before answering this question you should re-read Sections 6, 7 and 8.

This question is asking you to consider a historical interpretation about Cromwell's rule; firstly that it was a dictatorship and secondly that he was a 'willing dictator'. You must ensure that you do not allow your answer simply to become a recital of views but that you give a personal response. This response will:

- debate the issues surrounding the concept of dictatorship;
- incorporate the sources into the framework of your analysis.

Plan. To reach the highest level you need to plan your work accordingly. Most important of all you need to sustain an argument throughout the answer (see advice on page 103).

Style. The style of the answer should be one of synthesis, that is using the information from the sources to inform your analysis. Here is an extract from a model answer to the above question.

It is clear that a move to dictatorship went against Cromwell's deepest political instincts. The political stance taken in the 1640s in support of the Independents was never lost, merely compromised. Indeed this point is highlighted by Coward in Source C who stresses that Cromwell had never lost his 'Independent instincts for "healing and settling"'. That he could, in the 1650s, still show traits of such political instincts was, in part, due to his ideological schizophrenia, or what Wedgwood in Source B refers to as his being an 'enigma'.

BIBLIOGRAPHY

Alymer, G.E. *Rebellion or Revolution? England 1640–1660* (Oxford University Press, 1986)

Alymer, G.E. (ed.) *The Interregnum, The Quest for Settlement 1646–1660* (Macmillan, 1974)

Anderson, A. *The Civil Wars 1640–1649* (Hodder & Stoughton, 1995)

Ashton, R. *The English Civil War, Conservatism and Revolution 1603–49*, 2nd edn (Phoenix Giant, 1997)

Barnard, T. *The English Republic 1649–60* (Longman, 1982)

Bennett, M. *The English Civil War* (Longman, 1995)

Clarendon, E. Earl of *The History of the Rebellion and Civil Wars in England*, ed. MacCray (Oxford, 1959)

Coward, B. *Oliver Cromwell* (Longman, 1991)

Coward, B. *The Stuart Age – England 1603–1714*, 3rd edn (Longman, 2002)

Coward, B. and Durston, C. *The English Revolution* (John Murray, 1997)

Davies, G. *The Early Stuarts* (Oxford, 1959)

Firth, C.H. *Oliver Cromwell* (Oxford, 1900)

Fraser, A. *Cromwell our Chief of Men* (Weidenfeld & Nicholson, 1973)

Gaunt, P. *Oliver Cromwell* (Blackwell, 1996)

Gregg, D. *Politics, Religion and Society in Revolutionary England 1640–60* (Macmillan, 1989)

Gregg, P. *Oliver Cromwell* (Dent, 1998)

Hill, C. *God's Englishman* (Penguin, 1972)

Hirst, D. *Authority and Conflict* (Arnold, 1986)

Hutton, R. *The British Republic 1649–60*, 2nd edn (Macmillan, 2000)

Kenyon, J.P. *The Stuart Constitution* (Cambridge, 1966)

Leonard, A. *Oliver Cromwell* (Longman, 1998)

Lynch, M. *The Interregnum 1649–1660* (Hodder & Stoughton, 1994)

Mason, J. and Morrill, J. *Oliver Cromwell and the English Revolution* (Longman, 1990)

Morrill, J. *Reactions to the English Civil War 1642–49* (Macmillan, 1982)

Parry, R.H. (ed.) *The English Civil War and After 1642–1658* (Macmillan, 1970)

Paul, R.S. *The Lord Protector. Religion and Politics in the life of Oliver Cromwell* (London, 1955)

Reilley, T. *Cromwell an Honourable Enemy* (Phoenix Press, 1999)

Richardson, R.C. *The Debate on the English Revolution*, 3rd edn (Manchester University Press, 1998)

Richardson, R.C. (ed.) *Images of Oliver Cromwell* (Manchester University Press, 1993)

Roots, I. *The Great Rebellion* (Batsford, 1966)

Roots, I. (ed.) *Speeches of Oliver Cromwell* (Dent, 1989)

Seel, G.E. *The English Civil War and Republic 1637–1660* (Routledge, 1999)

Sharp, D. *England in Crisis 1640–60* (Heinemann, 2000)

Smith, D.L. *Oliver Cromwell: Politics and Religion in the English Restoration, 1640–58* (Cambridge University Press, 1991)

Smith, D.L. *Oliver Cromwell a Great Parliamentarian?* In Cromwelliana (Journal of the Cromwell Association, 1995)

Tomlinson, H. and Gregg, D. *Politics, Religion and Society in Revolutionary England 1640–60* (Macmillan, 1989)

Trevor-Roper, H.R. *Religion, the Reformation and Social Change* (London, 1967)

Woolrych, A. *Commonwealth to Protectorate* (Oxford, 1982)

Worden, B. *The Rump Parliament* (Cambridge, 1974)

Worden, B. (ed.) *Stuart England* (Phaidon, 1986)

Young, P. *Civil War in England* (Longman, 1981)

Young, P. and Holmes, R. *The English Civil War, A Military History of the Three Civil Wars 1642–51* (Eyre Methuen, 1974)

HEINEMANN ADVANCED HISTORY

INDEX